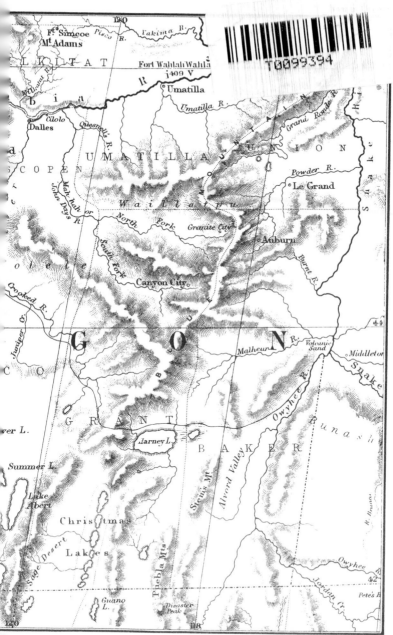

Ft Simcoe
Mt Adams
Pisco R.
Yakima R.

LKITAT
Fort Walilah Walilah
i 409 V

R
Umatilla

bia

Umatilla R.

COPEN
Cilolo
Dalles
Quesnelle R.
UMATILLA
Grand Ronde R.
MOUNTAIN
UNION
Powder R.
Le Grand

Mah Rah or
John Days R.
Wailatpu
North Fork
Granite City
South Fork
Auburn

Canyon City

Crooked R.
Burnt R.

G
O
N
Malheur R.
Volcanic Sand
Middleton

Juniper Cr
B
Owyhee R.
Snake

C
O

ver L.
G
R
A
N
T
B
A
K
E
R
Punash

Summer L.
Harney L.

Lake Abert
Steens Mt
Alvord Valley
R. Bruneau

Christmas
Lakes
Owyhee R.
Pueblo Mts

Sage Desert
Disaster Peak
Jordan Cr
Pete's

Guano L.

& Co.

Stanfords Geogl Establt London

OREGON:

THERE AND BACK IN 1877

OREGON STATE MONOGRAPHS

Studies in History

CLIFFORD TROW, *Consulting Editor*

OREGON:
THERE AND BACK IN 1877

BY

WALLIS NASH

FOREWORD AND NOTES BY

J. KENNETH MUNFORD

Corvallis:

OREGON STATE UNIVERSITY PRESS

Library of Congress Cataloging in Publication Data

Nash, Wallis.
    Oregon: there and back in 1877.
    (Oregon State monographs: Studies in history; no. 7)

    Reprint of the 1878 ed. published Macmillan, London; with new foreword, notes and bibliography.
    Bibliography: p. 290
    1. Oregon—Description and travel. 2. United States—Description and travel—1865-1900. 3. Nash, Wallis. I. Title. II. Series. F881.N24 1976   917.95 04′4   76-9770 ISBN 0-87071-077-X

FOREWORD

In *Oregon: There and Back in 1877*, Wallis Nash wrote to enlighten and to entertain, but he also had underlying purposes. As an English lawyer experienced in international financial matters, he had traveled to the west coast of North America representing a group of investors who were considering building a railroad. The line would run through an underdeveloped area that Great Britain had once claimed but from which it had withdrawn thirty years previously.

Nash wanted to tell prospective settlers that they would be welcome in a region that had land easy to acquire, rich and varied resources, and an expanding economy. He wanted to warn them of difficulties and hardships but to assure them of certain cultural advantages. He also wanted to entice bankers and businessmen to consider investment possibilities.

Nowhere in this sprightly promotional tract does the author stress these underlying purposes. He does not say why he and his companions came to Oregon, who paid their expenses, nor precisely what they were looking for. He gives only the briefest of introductions to the four principal participants. He usually refers to himself as "the lawyer" or "the artist," to Henry N. Moseley, F.R.S., as "the naturalist," to Francis E. Kerr as "the captain," and to T. Egenton Hogg as "the colonel."

In *A Lawyer's Life on Two Continents*, written many
years later, Nash tells how this group assembled and
describes the purposes of their journey. In the late spring
of 1877, he says, a friendly client recommended him to a
firm of French bankers who were interested in railroad
building and land grants in Oregon. Nash had represented
clients in many countries and had exceptional qualifications
for assisting the French investors in enlisting British capital
in their enterprise.

Two men, "an oddly assorted couple," Nash calls them,
came to see him at his office in London. One was "a stout,
suave, smiling" Parisian banker. The other was T. Egenton
Hogg, whom he describes as a former colonel in the Confederate army, "tall, lean, nervous, with curly brown hair,
a full beard, good forehead, large pale-blue eyes." Nash
recounts Colonel Hogg's description of himself:

> [Hogg] said that after the war, that left him a prisoner at
> Fort Alcatraz, in San Francisco Bay, he spent some time in
> hospital recovering fully from wounds and sufferings in war,
> and then he found himself at loose ends, all his property in
> New Orleans, where he was a merchant, having disappeared.
> He said that he had heard of large Government grants of lands
> in Oregon for road construction, and that, more to give him-
> self an object in his travels than with any definite ideas about
> values and possibilities, he had journeyed northward from
> San Francisco, being financed by his brother, a well-known
> Government contractor there; and, he added in a smiling
> parenthesis, as strong a Northerner as he was a Southerner.
> (*A Lawyer's Life on Two Continents*, p. 142.)

What Hogg proposed was that a railroad be built from
Yaquina Bay on the Oregon coast over the Coast Range,
through the "two prosperous towns, Albany and Corvallis,"
over the Cascade Mountains, and across eastern Oregon

to the Snake River and to a junction with a transcontinental railroad in Idaho.

Hogg told Nash how he had traveled over the lands that Congress had granted or would grant as a subsidy for the building of such a road. Hogg explained to Nash:

That the climate of the whole section was temperate and healthful; that there was abundant water, and that such parts of the grant as were included in the tract misnamed the Oregon desert in the maps of the day, would, when irrigated from the rivers issuing there from the Cascade mountains, prove to invite home making by thousands of new settlers. . . . At the close of an interview that had covered some hours the Colonel added that each section of the grants had special opportunities of its own, demanding opening out and developing. He was an interesting talker, evidently a man of foresight and imagination. (*A Lawyer's Life on Two Continents*, pp. 142-143.)

It was in 1871 that Colonel Hogg first visited western Oregon and began to take a hand in developing the railroad that had been started from Corvallis to Yaquina Bay. A toll road for wagons had already been opened as far as Elk City, on tidewater on the upper bay. Title to nearly 60,000 acres of land that had been granted as a subsidy for building of the wagon road had passed on to the Corvallis and Yaquina Bay Railroad Company which Hogg incorporated in 1872. Two years later, in 1874, Hogg incorporated the Willamette Valley and Coast Railroad Company for the purpose of extending a narrow gauge line into eastern Oregon.[1]

Enthusiasm for Hogg's project grew in London in 1877 as Nash arranged additional conferences with Hogg's associates and prospective investors. At one of them, Sir James Douglas, a former Governor of British Columbia

---

[1] See Harvey W. Scott, *History of the Oregon Country,* vol. 4, p. 330.

and at one time the officer in charge of the Hudson's Bay Company's operations in the Pacific Northwest, "verified all we had been hearing of the possibilities of settlement and population, and of the many industries which should there find development." It is easy to imagine the investors poring over maps Colonel Hogg rolled out on the table and the dreams of empire that infused the air.

They all realized that they needed "a new and full examination of and report on the territory in question before any action should be taken." Hogg and his financial partners agreed to pay the cost of such investigation. They invited Nash to select two other men to accompany himself and Hogg to Oregon.

Nash consulted Charles Darwin, his neighbor in Down, a village in Kent, 18 miles from London. Darwin recommended Henry N. Moseley, a Fellow of the Royal Society, to go along as a trained scientific observer. Moseley had recently returned from a four-year around-the-world oceanographic cruise on *H.M.S. Challenger* and had not yet completed his manuscript for *Notes by a Naturalist on the "Challenger"* (1879), but he readily accepted the invitation to join the investigators.

The fourth member of the traveling party was Francis E. Kerr of Melrose, a former captain who had "served the Queen long and passed some years in India."

Ready for adventure, these four left England in mid-June 1877, crossed the Atlantic and the American continent in 18 days, spent several days in and around San Francisco, and then went north into Oregon by riverboat, rail, and stagecoach. In Corvallis they rented horses to ride through the Coast Range areas where the land grants lay. Three others accompanied them to Yaquina Bay: George Mercer, a surveyor; E. A. Abbey, who served as a guide; and Colonel Hogg's brother William M., who spelled the family name *Hoag*.

After they returned to Corvallis, Nash and William Hoag went to see the Governor of Oregon in Salem, to visit the land office in Oregon City, and on to Portland. Colonel Hogg, Moseley, and Kerr followed the wagon road right-of-way east from Corvallis and Albany over the Cascade Mountains into eastern Oregon and then rejoined the others in Portland. On the return trip to California, they sailed down the Columbia River and along the Pacific Coast by steamship. They again crossed the continent by rail, this time through Niagara Falls and Ontario, Canada, and sailed for home from New York, arriving back in England about the middle of August.

In several places in the book reprinted herewith, Nash alludes, sometimes artfully, sometimes in an offhand manner, sometimes as straight reporting, to the railroad, to the compelling need for a deep-water port on Yaquina Bay, and to the prospects of success. On page 111 he casually mentions a railroad being built to provide "quicker and easier outlet from the [Willamette Valley] to the coast." On 121 he points out the potential superiority of Astoria and Newport as ports of the future. On 151 he comments on the ease with which Yaquina Bay could be converted into a deep-water port. On 246 he speaks again of "the superior claims of Yaquina Bay."

Moseley describes the prospects in more detail and with greater enthusiasm in his report of this trip, *Oregon: Its Resources, Climate, People, and Productions*. On page 81 he quotes the Surveyor-General of Oregon: "This road will tap the very heart of the Willamette Valley, and with its connecting lines throughout the State, and perhaps with one of the great transcontinental trunks of railway, will revolutionize the commerce of the country and open the floodgates of an immeasurable prosperity."

When Nash returned to London, he had no intention of ever leaving England permanently. A year and a half later he and his wife, Louisa A. Desborough Nash, surprised friends and relatives by announcing plans to emigrate to Oregon. Nash had been educated at Mill Hill School and New College, University of London. He had built a substantial and lucrative law practice in London and a reputation as an adviser on international investments. Why, friends asked, would anyone so well situated want to give up his career in Victorian England and move his family to the raw frontier of America?

Adventure, enterprise, and tragedy each had its influence.

The adventure of participating in the development of a new society appealed to Wallis Nash. He looked upon Oregon, a land but recently occupied by families of European descent, as "a clean sheet" on which imaginative leaders could write. "To one brought up among the fixed habits, ancient institutions, and permanent ideas of the old country," he says on page 207, "it is very interesting to see a community which has just had a clean sheet on which to inscribe its laws, its religion, its public and private education, its social habits." He grasped the opportunity to make marks on that sheet.

Another reason he had for moving to Oregon was to pursue the enterprise he had come to investigate in 1877. He was convinced by what he had seen and by what the Hogg brothers and others had to'd him that railroad building in that section of America had promising prospects.

The most immediate and urgent cause which brought the Nashes to the decision to leave England was a personal tragedy. As he described it many years later:

> No one could have had a happier home than I until some months after returning from my visit in 1877 to the Pacific Coast. Then, without warning the blow fell—virulent scarlet fever entered the nursery, and three victims were taken in a week. My wife [was] broken in health and spirit . . . life at Down had become impossible. . . . the question came to me . . . whether, at forty, we were still young enough to face removal from the old world to the new. . . . I found my wife a willing listener when I broached the subject to her. In the end we concluded to make our future home in Oregon. (*A Lawyer's Life on Two Continents*, pp. 154-156.)

In leaving England, the Nashes gave up friends such as their neighbors the Darwins; Sir Henry Bessemer, inventor of the steel-making process; and other "notables" of the time. The law firm of Nash and Field at No. 2 Suffolk Lane and 12 Queen Street had served a wide clientele— for example, the German banker who invented travelers' checks; leading actors of the day who were particular friends of Allan Field; Cyrus Field, the American who laid the Atlantic cable; a British company that purchased a sulfur company in Cesena, Italy, and another company that laid iron water mains in Genoa and recovered most of the cost of installation by selling as scrap metal the ancient Roman lead pipes which they dug up in the process.

Judah P. Benjamin, a one-time U.S. Senator from Louisiana who had been Attorney General and Secretary of State for the Confederacy, had escaped to England and joined Nash's firm after the Civil War and eventually became a Queen's Counsel.

When Alexander Graham Bell came to England to introduce the telephone, Nash represented him in obtaining British patent rights. The first long-distance call in England was made from Osborne, Queen Victoria's summer palace on the Isle of Wight, to Nash's office in London.

"A group of us listened in turn," Nash says, "as we distinctly heard for the first time the bugle that played at Osborne, *Home Sweet Home, Annie Laurie,* and other well-known strains. It fell to me to make arrangements with various business houses in London to introduce the telephone into their business life . . ."[2]

Leaving England was a hard decision for the Nashes to make—but Oregon profited immensely as a result. The railroad Nash and the Hogg brothers worked strenuously for two decades to build ended in bankruptcy, but the line they completed from Yaquina Bay through Corvallis and Albany eastward from there into the Cascade Mountains has served shippers along that route ever since and has become a valuable property of the Southern Pacific. Nash helped the Oregon Legislature frame railroad laws on uniform rates and other matters in the public interest. As a musician, artist, author, legal adviser, and Episcopalian, Nash influenced the cultural development of the mid-Willamette Valley. As an enthusiastic member of the Board of Regents of Oregon Agricultural College from 1885 to 1898, he helped provide a firm foundation for the development of Oregon State University.

After the Nashes moved from Corvallis to Portland in 1897, he continued to have an influence on the economy of the state as an attorney, as President of the Board of Trade 1906-1909, as the author of two handbooks for Oregon settlers, and as an editorial writer for Portland newspapers.

Nash was nearing 80 years of age when he retired to his ranch home near Nashville in the heart of the Coast

---

[2] A Lawyer's Life on Two Continents, p. 63. See also pp. 150-154.

Range. Thoughts of failure in the railroad venture caused a tinge of bitterness, but he also looked back on a full and exciting life and with gratification on his achievements. He had made indelible marks on Oregon's "clean sheet."

To assist the reader in identifying persons, places, and situations that might otherwise remain obscure, notes have been added to this facsimile reprint of Nash's 1878 book. An asterisk (°) in the text indicates that there is a note in the appendix identified by page number.

Many people have helped prepare this reprint edition. We appreciate their assistance. The efforts of James A. Blodgett and Gwyneth Britton are acknowledged in the Notes. Special thanks are also due Professor Roland E. Dimick and former Archivist Harriet Moore, both of Oregon State University, for their enthusiastic support. Harley Jessup rendered the map on page 283. Other illustrations are the pen-and-ink drawings from Mr. Nash's book.

J. KENNETH MUNFORD

Corvallis, Oregon
March, 1976

YAQUINA BAY—LOOKING TOWARDS LAND.

OREGON:

THERE AND BACK IN 1877.

BY

WALLIS NASH.

"All places that the eye of heaven visits
Are to a wise man ports and happy havens."
—*Richard II.*, i. 3.

London:
MACMILLAN AND CO.
1878.

PREFACE.

SINCE returning from the journey here described many questions have been put to me as to the climate, soil, productions, institutions, laws, and conditions of social life found on the Pacific slope, and chiefly in Oregon.

This proves that while there is a growing necessity for a better knowledge of that State, as her corn, wool, and salmon become more important articles of commerce, and on the other hand her applications for English manufactures are more loudly expressed, and the number of English settlers in Oregon is ever increasing, yet there is not available any simple and popular account of the State.

My visit, which resulted from a friendship of several years standing with Colonel T. Egenton Hogg—a Californian who has devoted the best years of his

b 2

life and a vast amount of energy, intelligence, and capital to acquiring extensive tracts of land in Oregon —convinced me that whilst English money is being, and will be, most profitably employed there, a field of emigration is also open which is suited in all respects to a large number of our fellow-countrymen.

Situated only twenty days journey from Liverpool,[*] possessing so many attractions in climate, soil, beauty of scenery, ease of access, freedom from drought, tempest, floods, and immunity from insect plagues, the next question which presented itself was whether the institutions of the State, its government, laws, and taxation, were such as to encourage the English settler.

My best answer to this appears in the following pages.

It is allowable for an Englishman to express deep regret that Oregon is not a British colony—that ignorance as to its capabilities and lack of faith in its future prevailed when it was ceded to the United States.

But it still can boast liberal laws, and the British settler, should he purchase and hold land and prosper in this State, will not find it necessary to abandon his British citizenship.

Should the reading of this book suggest to any to try their fortunes there, if they will communicate with me I will gladly put them in the way.

A handbook to Oregon, compiled from the best official sources, and verified by actual inquiry and observation, has been prepared by Mr. H. N. Moseley, M.A., F.R.S., the Naturalist to the late *Challenger* Expedition, who was one of our companions on this journey.

Reliable information is thus at the disposal of the intending settler.

I cannot end my pleasant labours in this book without gratefully recognising the kind reception we met in Oregon on all hands, from the Hon. S. F. Chadwick,* the Governor, to the little farmers in their cabins and the teamsters and herdsmen along the country roads.

WALLIS NASH.

BECKENHAM, KENT,
         March, 1878.

LIST OF ILLUSTRATIONS.

CONTENTS.

CHAPTER I.

CHAPTER II.

CHAPTER VI.

CHAPTER XII.

CHAPTER XIII.

OREGON.

OREGON.

CHAPTER I.

TRAVELLERS only can realise the thrill of excitement of climbing from the tender into the great White Star steamer as she lies in the Mersey, steam blowing off. In that one moment the regrets at leaving home, the fear lest human nature at sea should prove too weak, the joy of wandering, are strangely mixed.

But the pressing needs of finding one's cabin and getting "fixed" there, of preventing all the state-room luggage from being swept into the hold, of saying good-bye to friends who pity you for going so far away, and whom you pity for staying in the mill-wheel round of home duties, soon recall the first-time voyager to himself. As the ship passes from the dingy tide-water and "goes on ahead," and the ear gets accustomed to the rhythm and beat of the screw, which will unceasingly play the same tune for the next nine or ten days, we realise that the journey looked forwards to for years has begun.

The first night on shipboard passed, sea-life has fairly commenced. The passengers begin to make friends; neighbours at table comment on the meals; and the pace of the ship answers for that common topic, the weather, in ordinary landsmen's life. The afternoon after leaving Liverpool we reached Queenstown, to find the Channel fleet at anchor in the splendid harbour. One or two of the officers were shown over the *Germanic*, and praised the noble proportions of the ship, and the good order and cleanliness of every part. The eighth day after we left Queenstown we were nearing New York.

We had had three days of head-wind and sea, but had hardly known what rolling or pitching was: so that our preference for ships having state-rooms and saloons amidships, instead of aft, was justified. We had seen hundreds of porpoises, playing, rolling over, springing half out of the water, romping along; two whales had spouted for our amusement, the petrels had borne us company across the ocean, and now the Yankee gulls had come out to welcome us: very like,

only, we thought, a shade more lively even than their
Irish cousins who left us five days ago.

Now the excitement was to be certain if we could
get to the quarantine ground in New York harbour by
eight o'clock, that the health officers might come on
board to-night, and so suffer our hundred of American
passengers to spend their Sunday at home. Faster
and faster the ship went, until we were told, and we
believed, that for sixteen hours she had averaged
seventeen miles an hour. Long Island was in sight;
the lighthouse was passed; Sandy Hook was on our
left hand; and the ship stopped. The sudden silence
caused by the ceasing of that screw-beat, which had
registered fifty-two strokes a minute, and had formed
the unceasing accompaniment to so many tunes for
nine days, was almost oppressive.

The tug-boat, with health-officers, and with many
friends of the passengers on board, came in sight,
striking golden lights from the fast darkening waters
of the harbour, and in a minute the friendly groups
of the voyage were broken up: the quickly-made
acquaintanceships were as quickly ended. In a few
minutes the great ship seemed deserted, while cheer
after cheer sounded from the tug, crowded to the

gunwale, bustling along towards the city, the spires
and chimneys of which were shining in the sun's
last rays.

Having no special reason for hurry, the quartet
forming our party slept on board that Saturday night,
and only left the *Germanic* about eleven on Sunday
morning, after she had found her way, as neatly and
gracefully as a yacht, among the crowds of vessels, to
her berth alongside the White Star wharf.

The night before one of the custom-house officers
had remained on board, nominally to see that all was
right, practically to give all who were so minded the
chance of making to themselves friends of the Mammon
of unrighteousness.

It was a strange coincidence that the virtuous and
strong-minded passenger found it a tedious, complicated
matter to get, with his baggage, through the hands of
the officers in waiting on the wharf, while the old-
stagers, who in Rome did as Rome does, and were
busy as they left the ship in rolling dollar-notes into
the smallest compass, and then held them in the
lightest possible fashion in their fingers, passed quickly
through, baggage really unopened and unexamined, to
their carriages. Since we landed there have been great

changes in this matter, and there are new men, new manners—and quite time, too.

From the wharf a lumbering coach, swaying on its C-springs, took us to the hotel. But what paving! Holes here, ruts there, tram-roads everywhere! Our American travelling friend said, "You won't find worse roads in Oregon." We disbelieved him then; but he spoke the truth.

How hot it was! We bathed and dressed, putting on black coats and white ties, after the example of half the passers-by; but we had to change once more before the day was out: for every scrap of under-clothing on us was damp.

New York reminded us more of Continental cities than of English ones: so many trees shaded the side-walks; so many green jalousies were fixed outside the windows; while the absence of smoke and dirt on the house-fronts struck us all.

We were to travel West by the Monday evening train; so we ordered tickets from an agent sent by a friend who had passed West a day or two before, and who recommended him as active and prompt.

He was. He cheated us in the price of the tickets, in the collection and checking of the baggage, in the charge for sleeping-car berths. We should have saved money and temper had we shaken hands with him all round, given him cigars and drinks, and ourselves gone in a very expensive coach to the depôt of the railway to fetch our tickets ourselves. Was it not a really good introduction for simple-minded Englishmen? We congratulated ourselves that our teeth were fast in our heads, or they would have gone too. The American cities swarm with agents like our friend, who live (we cannot say they fatten) on strangers. At the railway and stage offices themselves, on the other hand, honesty and a certain rough, independent civility was the rule.

After some debate we settled to go West by the Pennsylvania railroad, going South from New York to Philadelphia, and thence West by way of Pittsburg and Fort Wayne to Chicago.

The train left at eight o'clock in the evening. About six our luggage was ready, and our first experience of the baggage-checking system began. Having each made up a hand-valise or carpet-bag of necessaries for the seven days' trip, everything else was to be "checked." The transfer company's agent came to the hotel with a bundle of brass labels on his arm, each label being attached to a leather strap with a loop, and bearing a plainly-impressed number, corresponding with a similar number on a small brass ticket. By the leather strap a brass label was looped on to each article of baggage, and the corresponding ticket handed to us. A small fee for each package was paid to the transfer agent. No one gave another thought to his baggage till we reached Omaha on the following Friday. The transfer company takes all trouble and risk of loss off the traveller's hands, and no one grudges the large dividends they earn.

Another institution we saw in full work. In the office of the hotel a small black case, like a travelling clock case, stands on the counter, by the clerk's side. A visitor wants a parcel carried to the other side of the city: the clerk touches an electric bell once, and in two minutes a bright, cleanly-dressed lad stands at the counter, waiting his instructions. In the same way a hack carriage is called, or a police-man summoned. The company which arranges all this supplies the battery and dial at a small annual charge, and the subscriber uses both as and when he pleases.

A still more useful novelty we noticed in full opera-tion at New York, and afterwards at Chicago and San

Francisco. This is the self-acting fire-alarm. In the
upper corner of every room and corridor of the hotel, in
many shops, offices, and warehouses, is fixed a modest-
looking dial-case, about five inches square. It is
hardly noticed as one enters the room. But day and
night a watch is kept. Let the temperature in the
neighbourhood of the little apparatus rise to 140
degrees, that is, let a fire break out in or near the room,
and the electric connection is automatically made, and
the alarm flashes to the nearest fire-engine station,
indicating the street, house, and room where the enemy
is at work. Here also the company owning the patent
receives a small annual sum, and supplies and keeps in
order the little machine.

About seven o'clock we had the family coach once
again, and rumbled and jolted to the Jersey City
ferry. In company with several other coaches and
waggons, and in a crowd of seventy or eighty
people, we got on to the huge ferry-boat really
without knowing it. We had parted from the land
and were well out in the stream before we saw that
we had started.

The machinery is hidden from the passengers'
view, and makes very little noise: the horses

were unconcernedly resting and blinking: passengers
were chatting, newsboys everywhere with the evening
papers, and in a few minutes we landed as easily
as we embarked, and took our places in the train.
Each place and berth in the long sleeping-car being
numbered and specially set apart previously for its
occupant, there was no scrambling or confusion;
and we were soon curiously scanning the faces of
our fellow-passengers, of whom we were to see so
much for the next seven days.

But it is time to label separately the members of
our party, since the experience of each on the
journey differed according to character, temper, and
history. It was a number of strange chances which
had brought together the naturalist, the captain, the
lawyer, and the American Confederate colonel. The
first had journeyed round the world and seen many
men, many manners; the second had served the
Queen long, and passed some years in India; the
third came straight from the worry and bustle of
London life; the fourth had travelled more than the
traveller, fought more than the soldier, schemed and
struggled more than the lawyer. When one man's
tongue was tired another took up the talk; and

when the three Englishmen gave in, the colonel was ready, with a fiery tale of the civil war, with incidents of prison life, with experiences in both hemispheres, with sporting life in Australia, India, and his native America, North and South—so that one way or other topics never failed.

The colonel left us by an earlier train to visit his friends in Baltimore and join our train in the night at Harrisburg—so the three Englishmen entered the train at eight alone : tickets they had for train and sleeping-berths; but their mentor having left them before the tickets were obtained, the firstfruits of the thieving agent's tricks appeared.

Showing their tickets, they asked for their places ; the negro porter pointed out one section for the four travellers : the two narrow seats below drawn out and joined made but one average-sized bed : the tray which was lowered overhead showed but one similar sized bed : so where were the four to sleep ? The agent had sold "berths" instead of "sections," thus giving but one half of the accommodation they supposed they were to get. Every other sleeping-berth in the Pullman cars was taken, so there was nothing for it but to draw lots

who should pass the night in the day-car: the
soldier ·lost, and so dozed, and smoked, and grizzled
all night long on the seats where one can neither
lie along nor rest.

Every one has heard described the cars, twice as
long as our English carriages, with passage down
the middle open throughout the train, and free
to "conductors," as the guards are called, and to
passengers of every grade in life.

But the scene as night comes on is strange. The
passenger calls the negro porter and tells him to get
the bed ready. Clearing the double seats of the
section of the books, bags, work, newspapers, and
any other litter with which they are strewed, the
porter drags the two seats together till they meet;
from the locker under each seat he draws pillows
and blankets; then reaching up, he turns a handle
in the sloping panel overhead and draws down a
shelf, forming thus the upper berth. There are
stored two mattresses and other bed clothes. Curtains
are slipped on to the rods running the length of the
carriage, and there are at once two rows of berths
completely curtained off the one from the other,
and the central passage through the car left clear.

Going to bed is a ticklish business. You disappear behind your curtains and roll into your lower berth or clamber into your upper one ; but what then ? Coats and waistcoats are easily doffed ; but there is only just room to sit, with feet stretched out : the position does not adapt itself to the farther operations of the toilet; consequently much agitation of the curtains and many grunts and groans disclose the sufferings of your neighbours. If you are in the upper berth, a smart shock from below shows you that the gentleman on the ground floor has not judged distance correctly with his head : if in the lower berth the shelf over your head creaks and groans till you expect a sudden fall in dry goods. Meanwhile the carriage rocks and tumbles along, and the Britisher is saying to himself, " Not much palace about this car — the line's *not* equal to the North-Western — talk of smooth travelling indeed ! "

But the longest night ends at last, and each traveller tries to forestall his neighbour at the washing-basins at the far end of the car. The porter puts away the beds, and the day is begun.

The morning after we left New York was lovely,

and we looked with curious eyes to mark the differences and resemblances between home and here. The fields were larger, the farming not so neat, more weeds, less grass; the hedges were absent, their places being taken by snake fences made of zigzag interwoven logs, seven logs in height, and each link in the zigzag about eight feet long.

Then the wooden houses with shingled roofs gave no idea of solid permanence to an English eye, but suggested rather the here to-day, there to-morrow, of a race always stretching forwards to new and better lands, and building and farming for themselves, and not for their grandchildren.

The nights were lighted with the fire flies dancing round every bush: the sunsets were resplendent with clouds of the deepest red.

Travelling on these lines even so far West as to Omaha is further made easy by the hotel cars attached to each train. Very cheap and excellent meals are served, and the hotel car is joined to the rear of the train from six in the morning till eight at night. The travelling kitchens are wonders of compact and clever stowage, and all the dishes of the season are served, with the pleasant accompaniments

of clean tablecloths and bright glass and silver, and
active, black-faced, white-jacketed waiters.

We passed Pittsburg, with its coal mines and
furnaces, the whole tract resembling the district
between Rotherham and Sheffield. The great
round-house at the station with its many engines,
each in its stall, waiting its turn for the road, was
a striking object; though we little thought how
soon it would be in flames, and one hundred and
one engines burned into shapeless twisted masses of
steel and brass in the labour riots, but a few weeks
after our visit.

After passing for many hours through undulating
country, with miles and miles of wheat and Indian
corn, dotted everywhere with farms, we approached
Chicago. The hills and rugged ground were
flattened out into wide fertile plains, and we got
our first glimpse of Lake Michigan.

The line approached the water: other lines met
and joined ours, several crossing at right angles on
the level: the masts of the shipping and piles of
lumber, with huge grain-elevators, showed us what
a centre of life and bustle we were entering: then
the train ran along the streets, the great bell on

the engine continually clanging to warn passers-by
off the unfenced railway, and we entered a dingy,
smoke-stained terminus.

The passengers and luggage going West were
transferred in omnibuses and waggons across the
city to the terminus of the Chicago and North-
Western line, and we found our way to an hotel
for a much-needed bath and breakfast.

As we crossed the city we· looked in vain for traces
of the fire.* The new buildings of brick and stone
surpassed those of New York in size and costliness ;
we passed a gap showing a lower level of three or
four feet, and were told that the whole city had been
rebuilt on this fresh-brought layer of soil, to raise
the streets and houses by so much above the level
of the lake. The streets were thronged like those
of Liverpool ; at the bridges in several places the
vehicles were formed by the police into lines to pre-
vent blocks ; the foot-passengers jostled each other
in crowds. A Chicago man in the train had told us,
" I guess Chicago is the most money-making city in
the United States ;" certainly it needed some attraction of that nature to overcome the drawbacks of

position on a perfect flat just on a level with the lake.

Two hours there sufficed us; and we were all glad enough to find our places for the next long stage in our journey—Chicago to Omaha.

CHAPTER II.

LEAVING Chicago about one o'clock by the Chicago and North-Western Line, we very soon lost sight of the lake and passed through an undulating, well-wooded and watered country for many miles. Then, crossing the Mississippi, we entered on vast plains of rich, dark soil, dotted everywhere with white farm-houses, each surrounded with its plantation of rapidly-growing cottonwood-trees. Wide-stretching fields of wheat, Indian-corn, clover, and oats reached as far from the railroad-line as we could see; and so across the State of Iowa.

Villages were growing up round every station; in each the church, the school, the liquor store, the black-smith's shop, and the store where agricultural machinery of all kinds was exposed for sale, were conspicuous.

Everywhere advertisements of the Buck-eye Reaper and the Champion Plough were displayed, and these

C

disputed every blank wall and fence with a notice of a knife-polish. The profits on the sale of this last must be stupendous, to judge by the outlay on this bill-posting extraordinary. Many hundred miles farther on, while passing through the wildest and grandest scenes, this ubiquitous knife-polish stared one in the face, and so accompanied us nearly from New York to San Francisco.

Mr. Mechi and Messrs. Moses and Son might learn many a lesson in this art from our American cousins. Here is a sample:—" Survival of the fittest. The ingenious doctrine propounded by Mr. Darwin, the tireless investigator of nature and her laws, is as applicable in determining the fate of medicines as in that of the animal species. Only those medicines which are best suited to the people's wants survive the test "—therefore buy Pierce's pills.

Nothing impressed so strongly on us the size of the United States as this ceaseless travelling through seemingly never-ending stretches of each kind of scenery. Gently rolling hills and dales lasted for days; broad, level plains covered with farms lasted for days; and now at last, after passing Omaha, we were to reach the prairie lands.

At Omaha, or rather at Council Bluffs, on the eastern side of the Missouri River, three lines converge, the Chicago and North-Western, the Chicago and Rock Island, and the Chicago, Burlington, and Quincy.

The Missouri is crossed by a bridge about three-quarters of a mile long, stretching high above the muddy brown stream, resting on lofty iron cylinders, with straight wooden and iron spans. As we looked up the river and across it and saw the thriving towns on each side, with factories, distilleries, machine-shops in full life and swing, it was hard to realise that thirty years ago the waggons of the pioneers were ferried across the river, while the emigrants rested in their tents by the river's side to recruit after the long stage passed, and take courage for the dangers and troubles of the plains and mountains still before them.

Here in 1846-7 the Mormon encampment was made on their way to their promised land ; and here, according to the Mormon records, Brigham Young enlisted five hundred of his followers for service in the United States Army in the Mexican War. From this point the Mormon battalions, with their waggons, started on their 2000-mile march, which carried them to San

c 2

Diego in California, "almost the entire march being over an uninhabited region, and much of the way a trackless, unexplored, and forbidding desert, affording neither water nor grass sufficient for the animals. When the teams failed, the battalion had to carry the extra amount of ammunition, and, at the same time, push the heavy waggons through the heavy sand and over the rugged mountains." [1]

At Omaha we reached the line of the Union Pacific Railway. A fresh train was ready to receive us, and all the baggage was re-checked. How the porters did rattle about the trunks! It was pitiful to see here and there a weakly one burst open with its fall, and all the poor treasures of the emigrant exposed to rough usage and loss. The safest packages were the huge, round-topped, iron-bound coffers, called Saratoga trunks. In each corner of the bottom is cunningly hidden a metal roller; the trunk is too heavy for the porter to lift, drag it he must; so the rollers save the corners from the wrenching which looks violent enough to rend any ordinary box into pieces.

The great shed was a scene of the wildest confusion.

[1] *Rise, Progress, and Travels of the Church of Jesus Christ of Latter-Day Saints.—Deseret News* Office, Salt Lake City.

The baggage-car was drawn up at one door, and down a slide to the floor followed an unending string of every named and unnamed piece of luggage. The number of the label on each was shouted by a porter as it left the car; the number was registered in a book by another man; the passengers, lining a rail across the shed, each claimed their own property, and handed over their corresponding labels. Their destination was then demanded, fresh labels issued to them, the luggage was weighed, and excess paid for, and the passengers were free to take their seats in the cars which were to carry them to Ogden Junction.

Excess luggage is a serious matter. From our party of four, forty-three dollars was demanded and paid; not without a lively passage of arms between the colonel and a very meddlesome porter, whose mistaken view was that he was entitled to divide up the luggage of the party amongst its four owners, two of whom had considerably less than the one hundred pounds allowed, and so surcharge the colonel with the whole excess incurred by his weighty trunks, laden with outfit and accumulations of a year's foreign travel. But justice, and the colonel, prevailed; our trunks and bundles, gun-cases, and "fish-poles" were heaped together on the weigh-bridge, and forty-three dollars was the charge. Let future passengers profit by this hint.

In a small office in the station at Omaha the agent was placed for the sale of the railway company's lands in the State of Nebraska. It was furnished with samples of all kinds of grain and hay grown in the State, with a label on each, stating by whom it was grown, when planted, and when harvested. We counted upwards of 320 grains of Indian-corn on one cob. Other samples were as prolific. The handbooks for emigrants were got up in first-rate style, with numerous pictures. To be led by them would be to believe Nebraska to be the most fertile, prosperous, and enjoyable State in the Union—the severity of its winters, the violence of the winds sweeping its vast plains, were passed by in silence.

Soon after leaving the station at Omaha the farms cease, houses are left behind, and the line, gradually rising from the 966 feet above sea-level at Omaha, by slow stages mounts to 8,242 at Sherman Station, the highest point on the route. We ran by the side of the Platte River for upwards of 340 miles, parallel most of the way with the great overland trail, the

route of the early emigrants to California, as well as
that of the Mormons to Salt Lake. It is a well-worn,
dusty track, even yet used by occasional waggon-
trains.

White-tilted, narrow waggons, on high wheels, were,
even as we looked, being dragged sluggishly by fourteen or sixteen oxen each, and alongside his slow-
pacing team the leader of the expedition trudged with
his long whip, dust everywhere rising in clouds.

About eight months, one old lady afterwards told
us, it had taken her, with her husband and children,
to get across from Missouri to California, the average
day's journey being six to eight miles, and rests being
often needed for several days, in grassy spots, to recruit
the oxen. They travelled in company for protection
from the Indians, but often had to go hungry to bed,
the provisions running short. In those days, the
buffalo ranged these prairies in bands of many
thousands each. Nowadays the few survivors have
moved hundred of miles away from the railway, with
its clanging bell and howling whistle.

The most striking feature of this prairie-travelling
was the absence of all boundaries. Neither hedge,
nor fence, nor road, nor line of trees was in sight,

and the vast grass-covered undulations stretched away
till the nearer features became quite indistinguishable
in the limitless distance.

But the land had a wild beauty of its own; the grey
of the long sun-burned grass was soft indeed; the
gentle undulations of the plains led the eye away till
the near grey faded into the distant blue, while here
and there a band of antelopes stood boldly out against
the sky.

They seemed too tame for their own comfort. Often
they were within range of the train, and there was a
perfect fusillade from the rifles and revolvers with
which a good many of the passengers were armed.

A travelling New York company of actors specially
distinguished themselves. All day long their firearms
were popping at objects, live or dead; if antelopes,
prairie dogs, and jackass rabbits did not show themselves, any conspicuous stone or rock, within reach,
served to draw their fire; and they were deaf to all
the remonstrances of their more peaceable and sober-
minded fellow-travellers. Not that any of the living
marks were any the worse, so far as we saw; for invariably they bounded off, or turned somersaults into
their holes, unhurt.

Occasionally the whistle sounded loudly and vehemently, to frighten, from the unfenced railroad track, a herd of the half-wild cattle, of which thousands pass the summer months on these prairie lands, being driven eastward, in slow stages, until the limits of cultivation are reached, when they are packed tightly into railroad cars, to finish their journey to the Eastern States.

Here and there, in a hollow of the prairie, were one or two waggons, with picketed horses round, and often a drove of unbroken colts and fillies ; the camp fire was the centre, round which four or five picturesque figures were grouped. These men start in the early spring from the far western plains with a great band of cattle or horses, and finish their journey only in the autumn months.

Always rising, we passed the border of Nebraska and entered Wyoming. The train stopped at Cheyenne, a town of 6,000 inhabitants, planted there 6,000 feet up on the Rocky Mountain slope, with no trees to shade it, no hedges to break the rush of the wind.

Soon after crossing Dale Creek Bridge, 650 feet long and 126 high, we came to the coal-bearing district appropriately called Carbon. From these mines the Union Pacific locomotives are supplied. There is

a little town of huts half-sunk in the ground, in which
the miners live. The piles of coal stored there indicated a large output.

The first snow-fences and snow-sheds are now seen.
The former, running at an angle from the line for several
hundred yards, stop the drifting of the snow; the latter
are wooden tunnels, made of sturdy beams and trunks
of fir-trees, each snow-shed being watched by a man,
whose business it is to pass through after each train
and guard against the fires, which have often destroyed
in an hour the fruit of months of labour and hundreds
of dollars expenditure. A lonely life, often miles from
his station and house, with no excitement save the
six trains which generally pass in each twenty-four
hours : the Western Pacific express, the Atlantic Eastern
express, two emigrant trains, and two freight or luggage
trains.

For many miles the level of the rails was being, or
had been, raised from three to eight and ten feet, and
this work was carried on without stopping the traffic.
Huge ploughs drive deep furrows into the soil on
either side of the road, and loosen it. Then great
scrapers follow, and the earth is piled on to the line.
Then the ties (*Anglicè*, sleepers) are raised, with the

metals attached, and the work on that spot is done. And this is found the best protection against the winter snowdrifts.

Then, after passing the boundary of Utah, the scenery gradually changed. The land became more undulating; the grey, withered grass of the prairie was sprinkled and broken with rocks, and, after a barren stretch, we reached the limits of the Mormon cultivation.

Small farmhouses reappeared, some brickbuilt; each surrounded with its plantation of trees, its garden and orchard. Rills of running water were led everywhere through the fields, carrying fertility with them. Fruit-trees appeared, and luxuriant fields of lucerne[*]and clover. At the stopping-places children brought jugs of cider to sell to the thirsty passengers.

Many of the houses bore the Mormon sign, an open eye, surrounded by rays, with their motto, "Holiness to the Lord." Soon we reached the junction, at Ogden, with the Salt Lake City line, and changed into the cars of the Central Pacific road. Turning North, the line skirts the Great Salt Lake.

As we saw it, a more lovely scene the eye never rested on. The fore-shore of the lake was green with

grass and weed, with lines of shining water everywhere
catching the evening light. The sun, sinking towards
the snowy range of mountains on the Western side of
the lake, sent quivering rays across its waters, while
purple and orange clouds were piled up high above
the horizon.

Flocks of white waterbirds were everywhere taking
flight as the train startled them from their evening
rest, and in long lines sought fresh beds farther along
the shore. One or two of the Mormon settlers were
gathering in the herds of cattle, which, during the
day, had been feeding on the succulent grasses of the
flat lake shore ; and, as night drew on, we left cultivation behind, and were again threading our way among
a maze of rocks and low mountains, the line winding
here and there, seeking the smoothest passage
through.

The next day was the dreariest and hottest of the
trip. We had passed into Nevada. The stations were
sometimes piled with stacks of silver ingots, and the
platforms were thronged with miners, some in the
workaday costume of dingy, earth-and-water-stained
trousers tucked into unblacked knee-high boots, with
flannel shirts of every hue ; others in the Sunday

garb of black cloth pantaloons, fine white linen em-
broidered shirts, with diamond pins and rings.

One tall fellow in the height of fashion, with a
silver bracelet round one arm, between shoulder and
elbow, outside a spotless white shirt, and carrying the
other arm in a sling, entered our smoking carriage,
and told us how three days before a mass of earth
had fallen on him in the mine, and, he believed, had
dislocated his left shoulder, and how. he was going
down to San Francisco to get the surgeon's help.

We followed down the course of the Humboldt River.
It wound along with a slowly flowing stream, its banks
lined with alders and cotton-wood, taking in affluents
here and there, and growing wider and stronger, till
it spread out into a marshy plain,—and then appeared
no more. It sank away into the sand. We lost sight
at once of water and greenness, and the sage plains,
white alkali-covered stretches dotted over with the
grey sage bush, were the only prospect.

A white impalpable dust filled the air and entered
the carriages, even through the carefully closed double
windows and shut doors. It settled on everything,
our faces included. Wherever it lay on the skin it
made it hard, tense, and sore. If washing was tried

the skin cracked, eyes got bloodshot and hot; and
we passed some hours of misery, the sun streaming
down, with no breath of wind to moderate its
power.

The only living thing visible in these wastes was
an occasional jackass rabbit lazily loping among the
bushes, and one or two large hawks circling high
overhead. Here and there, before we lost sight of the
Humboldt River, we saw an Indian camp, and at every
station some of the miserable squaws and children
came to the train to beg; while their lords and
masters, in the cast-off clothes of the white men,
with a gaudy blanket draped round the shoulders
of each one, squatted under the shadow of the station
fence, or lounged along the platform.

Their miserable shanties were not worth the name
of huts: a few bushes stuck in the ground, with one
or two longer sticks supporting an old ragged blanket
or cloak. Here and there a raw-boned pony was
tethered, standing with drooping head and tail, the
image of laziness and despair. The dirty, haggard,
unkempt squaws had no English words to beg with,
and mutely held up their hands, sometimes with a
battered meat-tin or broken pot, for the fragments

of bread and meat and half-eaten fruit which were thrown to them from the windows of the train.

These people are the survivors of tribes which disputed, with hundreds of braves, the incoming of the white men; and several of the stations bear names recording battles and skirmishes in which many an emigrant, and many a soldier too, fell. The alder-bushes often covered many acres by the river-side with a thick shrubbery.

One of these thickets was the scene of an adventure described to us by the chief actor in it.

Some few years ago, in the height of the Indian wars, our friend had to travel alone on horseback from one of the United States forts to another with dollars he was collecting as the price of the corn and other provisions with which he supplied the troops.

Night closed in after a seventy miles' ride, and he dismounted, picketed his horse to feed, and eat his frugal supper of biscuit and bacon, not daring to light a fire, lest it should betray him to Indian enemies. Then leading his horse into the heart of the shrubbery, he tethered him there, and lay down, his head on his saddle, and wrapped in his blankets, for a few hours' rest.

He had not slept long, when he was awakened by hearing voices near. He lay and listened, recognising Indian talk. Softly unrolling himself from his blanket, he held his rifle and revolver ready and soon saw the light of a fire but a few yards off

Creeping softly nearer, he made out three Indians crouching, after their fashion, round a few burning sticks. The Indians despise the huge camp fires of the white men. They say, "Make small fire, can get close to it : big fire keep you away, no good."

The Indians had, like himself, no thought but of hiding in the thicket to sup and sleep. He heard their horses near by cropping the branches, and dreaded the moment when his own horse would discover other horses near, and neigh for company.

He dared not wait till the Indians had finished their supper and laid down to sleep; so he crawled back to his own horse—fortunately his friend—expecting every moment that some unlucky movement would make noise enough to rouse the attention of his most unwelcome neighbours.

But fortune smiled on him; he found his horse calmly waiting his return. Quietly he saddled him, and cut the rope he dared not attempt to draw in

and coil.   Jumping on his back, he charged through
and over the Indians at their fire, which lay directly
in his road to the open ground.   Startled by the
unlooked-for rush, they scattered deep into the
bushes, not knowing how many foes they had to
reckon with; and in a second he was galloping, far
out in the clear, dark night, over the open prairie,
thankful indeed for an unhoped-for escape, and
fearing no pursuit.

Soon we crossed the Washoe range of hills, and
neared the boundary of California.   The railroad line
began to climb the foot hills of the Sierra Nevada.
The grey sage-bush plains disappeared, and the pine-
trees of the Sierra took their place.   The air grew
clear and bright, and we all breathed freely once again.

A fellow-traveller of ours told us how, three years
ago, he was snowed up for three weeks in February
at one of these stations.

Knowing that such an event was possible, he and
his friends had provisioned their sleeping-car with
preserved meats and soups, huge tins of crackers
(*Anglicè* biscuits), abundance of jams and marmalade,
and plenty of champagne.

The train, with six engines, crept slowly up towards

D

the summit, charging successfully through several drifts ; but the snow lay deeper and deeper as they mounted.

They stopped for water at a little town, with one small inn, two saloons, and two stores. They started, but soon came to a standstill, the engines buried deep in the drift ; the train backed, and again and again they charged the wall of snow, but only got so far in as not to be able to back out again, and there they stuck.

The next day they tried again to get through, but were defeated : the snow continued to fall, and they were forced to give up all idea of getting forwards till an army of diggers could be sent to clear the way. Backwards was equally impossible, as they were cut off from help by many miles of snow, ever growing deeper.

After two days the provisions in the other cars began to fail. The passengers, many of them miners on their way to San Francisco for a spree, began to grumble at the plenty reigning in the Pullman car; but laid siege to the inn and the saloons in the station-town, and were quieted. The cold at night was intense, and the fuel in the train began to fail.

There were three ladies in the Pullman car—one
old and two young—so the gentlemen persuaded
them to move their quarters to the inn; and, after
a struggle through four hundred yards of snow, they
succeeded in reaching their port of refuge. They
found the inn full of miners and rough customers
from the other part of the train, who were willing
to receive the ladies and give them shelter, but
hesitated to admit their male companions; high
words followed, and the presence of the ladies alone
kept the peace.

The next day they thought it prudent to get back
to the Pullman; so loading themselves with as many
billets of wood as they could carry, they made their
painful way back to the train, settled in the snow.
But soon the mob from the inn followed, and tried
to force an entrance into the car. The ladies
shrank into a corner, while the gentlemen held
the doors and windows against all comers; and so
followed a free fight, ending in the assailants being
beaten off. This was renewed once and again. In
the end a treaty of peace was made, the provisions
in the Pullman car were shared among the passengers,
regardless of original rights, and harmony reigned.

In the evening all parties adjourned again to the
inn; songs were sung, stories told, punch brewed,
and the ladies bivouacked by the inn-parlour fire.
This life lasted for three whole weeks, and the last
of the preserved meats and biscuits were being
eaten, when the rescuing army of Chinamen cut
their way to the snowed-in train.

Twenty miles of snow-sheds now secure the
winter traffic from this kind of interruption but we
heard how last winter eleven engines to one train
of cars were employed to force a passage.

Ever since we entered at Ogden, on the Central
Pacific line, the labourers on the line were Chinese.
Every few miles we passed a group of five or six
celestials, straw-hatted, blue-clothed, and long-tailed
—their faces burned from the natural olive to a
healthy brown—holding shovels with handles six
feet long; making up, by the patient, tireless hand-
ling of their tools, for the small spadefuls they raised
at each stroke.

Here and there a barrack-looking house stood by
the roadside where they lodged, with numbers of
them off duty hanging about the doors, smoking
their pipes and chatting; looking too many for the

house to hold. The sight of the lodging-houses in China Town in San Francisco, though, explained matters, and showed us how ten Chinamen herd together in a space where three Europeans would be stifled.

And at the stopping-places for meals we now were waited on by China boys. In short white linen frocks, their long tails tightly wound round their heads, they flew here, there, and everywhere round the room: intent on their own duty, they took not the slightest notice of the various commands and intreaties of individual passengers till all were served. Then John condescended to bring a glass of water or of milk, and even to secure for a very polite passenger a second helping of peach or apricot pie.

The absence of wine, beer, or spirits at all meals was very noticeable to the English passenger. Tea and coffee were served invariably at breakfast, dinner, and supper. If drinks were wanted, the saloons were open, and naturally a good many adjourned there at odd times; but iced water was the prevailing beverage.

We climbed the Sierra Nevada proper in the

night. We were roused soon after two to catch a glimpse of Lake Donner, lying almost hidden among the mountains, the moon shining brightly on its still waters, and the solemn pine-trees standing round its brink.

As day dawned we were quite among the mountains—like no others that we had seen before—in their steep, pine-covered sides, light-grey colour, and serrated, broken tops. We were now in the heart of the mining district.

The characters and scenes of Bret Harte's Californian sketches passed before us.* Truckee, Red Dog, Bloomer Cut, You Bet, Cisco, Gold Run, Dutch Flat, Poker Gully, lay in turn in the sunshine. Flumes (timber-made and supported sluices) ran by the line for miles; the country was turned up, seamed, scarred, stripped, broken; hill-sides washed down into the valleys; valleys choked with spoil and refuse, holding here and there a hut, with no approach save over heaps of water-worn gravel.

At each station Tennessee and his partner, Henry York, Sandy McPherson, Colonel Starbottle, and the rest, were all diligently employed in doing nothing. We had seen some feeble attempts at laziness before :

the emigrants on the steamer deck; the Irish in the low
streets of New York.   The Indians in Utah were lazy.

But for the height, the very perfection, of this art of
doing nothing, show us a saloon in a mining district, in
the afternoon, with a deep verandah running along the
front, next a dusty road; a bright bare sunny sky overhead, no wind; five or six chairs under the verandah,
each tilted on its two hind legs, with a sallow, pointed-
bearded, felt-hatted, shirt-sleeved, black-trousered, long-
legged individual in each; two out of five smoking, and
three out of five chawing; three out of five hands deep
in trousers-pockets; two out of five gently whittling
away at splinters of wood with long sharp knives.

Go and stand by and smoke, and try to be lazy
yourself: it is not bad: never speak: if you are asked
a question in the course of a quarter of an hour,
don't answer, only grunt; unless a man on a tilted
chair says slowly, "What'll you drink, Mister?"
Then say, equally slowly, "Guess a cocktail 'll do me,
you bet."   But don't refuse; each lanky idler has got
a pistol in his trousers-pocket, loaded, and they do go
off so easily.

California is a land of fruit; the most unlikely-looking
folk came to the train to sell as the day wore on; old

mulattoes, young and sprightly boys (whose idea of a
joke was for each to run off with his neighbour's choicest
peach, just as he believed he had secured a buyer); old
worn-out miners; but no women old or young.

Peaches, figs, strawberries, plums, grapes, cherries,
were in profusion at each station; for one "bit," say
fivepence, a basket of cherries or strawberries, holding
more than one person could eat, was offered.

Then we reached Cape Horn. The mountains were
tumbled and tossed in the wildest confusion. The line
wound backwards and forwards, always climbing up.
We passed the boldest tressel bridge we had yet seen.
Spanning a deep gully, it was built up of tiers of
wooden beams interlaced and tied together; so high
that it was guyed by wire ropes anchored into the hill-
sides, to take off the strain of the wind in times of storm.

The engine slackened to four miles an hour, and we
passed gently across, the wood creaking and groaning
as the weight was felt. The cattle feeding below
looked the size of sheep, and the man driving them
a pigmy. And then clinging to the mountain side,
along a narrow ridge, we passed to the highest point.
Rounding a bluff, the train stopped, the passengers got
out, and we gazed almost fearfully down 2,000 feet into

the valley, which we all but overhung. At the bottom the American River, which is a considerable stream, looked but a thread, the tall pines but tiny plants.

The Chinese navvies who built this road were hung in ropes from above, each with his pickaxe, till he could hew a footing for himself, and then by slow degrees the shelf on which the track is laid was cut from the rock.

Running rapidly down the mountains, we reached Sacramento, the capital of the State, a city of 40,000 people. The Capitol, a lofty, domed building, in the Italian style, stood conspicuous, shining in white marble, stone, and stucco. The streets were lined with stores, having continuous verandahs, most necessary in the broiling sun.

Then broad corn-fields, studded with fine oak-trees, stretched for many miles. The wheat had been reaped or harvested; it was being thrashed out in the fields; steam-thrashing machines were everywhere at work, and by each was the pile of bags of wheat, and the huge heap of straw shortly to be burned. Large bands of horses in the fields, from which the corn had been cleared, standing under the shade of the oak-trees, showed why so many trees were left.

The ground was scored here and there by the
burrows and runs of the grey ground-squirrels, or
gophers, which were running merrily about; and
plenty of jackass rabbits (of the size of hares, and
with even longer ears), gave promise of sport for the
greyhounds which are now common in the State.

As the evening drew on, and we got near our
journey's end, troops of friends of the passengers joined
the train at each station, and many pleasant family
greetings were seen. Acquaintances of the journey introduced each other to their relatives, and the English passengers were not left out. Californian hospitality showed
itself at once, and invitations were plentifully given.

Then we moved slowly through the town of Oakland,
the engine bell warning trespassers off the line, and
the train ran out on the long timber staging jutting
far out into the bay.

The salt water plashed round the piles; the sea
breeze came in fresh and cool. We entered the great
ferry-boat in waiting at the end of the jetty, in which
boat all the passengers in the train were taken in, with
room for plenty more. We moved rapidly away towards
San Francisco, lying on the opposite hills, with the
sights and sounds of a great city ever growing nearer.

The ferry boat passed neatly into its berth among
the shipping, and we landed among a crowd of
gesticulating, yelling hotel touters and porters, each
with the name of his hotel shown in gilt letters on
his cap.   We found the Lick-house family coach in
waiting, and were jolted over the roughest of paving to
the hotel, glad enough to be at rest after 3,000 miles
of sea and 3,000 miles of land safely passed in
eighteen days. *

UTAH INDIANS.

CHAPTER III.

A FEW hours sleep in California refreshes one. The
night breeze is always cool; in the height of summer
two blankets are wanted on the beds; the air is invigorating, full of life. As you pass along the streets
of San Francisco, the passers-by look brisk, eager,
active-minded, and alert, often worn with worry and
excitement, but giving no evidence of rumination
or rest.

How proud the inhabitants are of their city! Built
on hilly ground, fronting towards the north and west,
with the waters of the bay washing the end of every
street, it cannot be other than a healthy place.

Everywhere fine buildings of granite and stone are
displacing the original wooden houses, and these last,
if in good condition, are not pulled down, but moved
off bodily into the suburbs. As you pass along the
wide streets, the look ahead is blocked up by a house

in the middle of the road.   Going near, you find a
wooden house set on rollers, being wound up by a
horse moving round a capstan to an anchor fixed into
the road.   After a journey of say fifty yards, the
anchor is moved another stage forwards, and the
house slowly but steadily follows.   Meanwhile passing
carriages have to get by as best they can; no one
objects to the annoyance, for what his neighbour is
doing to-day, it may be his turn to undertake to-
morrow.

As soon as the English visitor has delivered his
letter of introduction, and often on the strength of
an acquaintanceship formed on the journey there, the
San Franciscan invites his friend to a drive to the Cliff
House to breakfast.

Rising at six the next morning, you find at the hotel
door a light buggy (with wheels looking as fragile and
slender as if a bicycle, and not a carriage, had been
in the builder's mind), with a pair of spirited blood
horses.

Mounting beside the driver, you pass slowly at first
over the uneven streets till you reach the outskirts,
and pass palace after palace of a style of building
peculiar to the place.

Marble steps outside lead up to a porch, laid with encaustic tiles, forming the entrance to a lofty house, always white, covered with carved-work framing in each door and window. Plate-glass in every window, but all the house of wood. The rooms are large, light, commodious, well furnished. Each house is surrounded with a little garden full of bright flowering shrubs and flowers; but its chief glory is a terrace or slope of the greenest turf, shaven close, and constantly watered.

Then you reach the Park.* Here is art triumphing over nature. Outside its limits are hills of loose drifting sand, on which no green thing grows. Within its boundaries soil has been painfully carted in, then planted with a lupin, which is the only plant which, for the first year or two, can struggle against the clouds of sand brought up by every wind.

But then firs of all kinds, laurels, laurustinus, heaths, arbutus, were planted, and, being constantly watered, thrive well.

The hollows were filled with water, and lakes thus formed. The roads, gravel laid, and rolled, and well watered, are tempting to charioteers whose passion is fast driving, and constant notice-boards are needed,

ROCKY MOUNTAINS, SUMMIT—CENTRAL PACIFIC RAILWAY.

SEAL ROCK, NEAR SAN FRANCISCO.

by which speed in the Park is limited to ten miles an hour. Outside and beyond the Park similar level stretches, with no limit as to pace, lead between the sand hills ; and so past the great cemetery, called Lone Mountain, to the beach, and our drive ends by half a mile over the hard, smooth sand, with the breakers of the Pacific rolling in on our left, and before us the picturesque and rugged rocks forming the southern doorpost of the Golden Gate.

The Cliff House is built on a rocky ledge, with its verandah looking straight out to sea, and there, while the oysters and tender-loin steak are being got ready, we make acquaintance with the sea-lions.

One large and two smaller rocks are their home, the larger dotted over with the unwieldy brown beasts, basking in the sun. They climb painfully to the highest points, and seem to play "I'm king of the castle" continually, though none of average size care to try conclusions with one huge overbearing brute, with a scarred chest, commonly known as Brute Butler.

When the fancy seizes them, splash they go from the rocky points into the pure green water below, exchanging in a moment their lumbering crawl on the rock for the graceful, agile, swift motions of the seal.

After twisting, waltzing, gambolling to their hearts'
content, they emerge sleek, black, and dripping on to
the lower rocky ledges, and then up again they climb
into the sunshine to dry.

What a happy life! Protected by law, and custom,
and public opinion from any cruel, thoughtless shot.
Well-fed, well-lodged, and with daily changing spectators of their feats to minister to their vanity (if sea-
lions are vain ; and surely they are as they twist their
long bodies into attitudes, and turn their great soft
eyes towards the balcony side of their rocks).

John Chinaman must envy them. As our host
observed, " It would be far safer for a rough to kill
a Chinaman than one of them, for, if one were shot
at and hurt, the rascal's life would not be worth an
hour's purchase."

After a good " square " meal, earned by early
rising, and done full justice to by appetites sharpened
by the crisp, bright sea-breeze, we turn the horses'
heads towards the city, some five miles off.

The road is smooth, and not too hard ; the horses
tearing at their bits with impatience ; our driver, with
a rein in each hand, plants his feet firmly, and we
are off.

A dozen similar vehicles, bent on a trial of speed, start with, or just behind, or before, us. Our friend says calmly, "Not a three-minute pace yet; we shall do a two-fifty gait presently." The horses settle down into a lunging far-reaching trot, with action not high, but long. Presently a rival steals up alongside, and is all but passing as our friend is chatting and not driving.

He holds his horses tighter, and very decisively, but not too loud, the looked-for " G— along " is heard, and then they step in real earnest. Faster and faster the other team presses on us, and presently, there being no passenger in that buggy, they go by; but the pace is tremendous. After a couple of miles of real racing we pull up by degrees, and soon pass the racecourse, where we stop to see the training of the trotters for the public races going on. Five or six horses, each in front of a huge pair of wheels, with a little seat wedged in between them, on which the driver sits, almost on the horse's back, were being carefully timed round the mile track.

By this time it is nearly ten o'clock, and we soon, at a sober pace, enter the city again, before the wind rises, as it soon will do, to make the road a purgatory of dust.

Our party scattered, each to his own pursuits. The naturalist went off to see a collection of the minerals of the Pacific coast, and to hear full details of the Lick University trust.

If money and judgment and determination will do it, the trustees will succeed in getting together a staff of professors to do honour to the intentions of the founder, who set aside the fortune, earned by a long life of industry, to provide the means of the highest education for the youth of the State to which he owed his own success.*

Nothing is more striking than the determination of these recently-settled States to plan and foster the colleges and universities which seem as necessary a part of their public life as the capitol and the court-house.

Land is freely set aside to provide the funds. Teachers are plentiful. Students of both sexes flock in; and so in stores, on farms, in sawmills and factories, on river steamboats, and on stages, you find roughly-dressed, plain-looking youngsters, who cut their mother tongue to tatters in their common talk, but whose knowledge is not contemptible of mathematics, history, mechanics, chemistry, geography, and who would be generally competent to take a fair place in the modern school at Harrow, Winchester, or Marlborough.

Having introductions to brothers of the craft in San Francisco, the lawyer found his way to the court-house, where the circuit court of the Supreme Court of the United States was holding special sittings, to try a mining case from Nevada, where two great companies were claiming the same vein of silver ore.

Three judges were on the bench in a lofty but not large court, distinguishable merely by their place of honour, but not by wig and gown; below them sat the registrar and clerks, and then came the table on which the attorneys engaged in the case had placed their briefs and books; then the body of the court, filled indiscriminately with attorneys, witnesses, and public. The proceedings were dignified and decorous, though wigs and gowns were absent, and there were no distinctions between Queen's Counsels in silk and the outer bar in stuff, and the solicitors in the purgatorial well below, and no crier and usher with his "Silence, silence!" when the murmur of voices gets too loud.

The walls of the court were hung with great maps

and sections of the ground in dispute, and the case was farther illustrated by a large glass model, showing through its transparent sides transverse sections of each distance of fifty feet on the lode in dispute, painted on the glass slips filling the case.

The case was fully argued, as became the magnitude of the issues involved, and so far as an entirely un-prejudiced and disinterested witness could judge, neither litigant could have cause to question the industry and ability of the attorneys who argued, of the witnesses who supported and assailed the respective views of the attack and defence, or the care and independence of the judges, who seemed to let no point slip.

There was one moment in the hearing strange to an English eye, when, to elucidate some point, judges, witnesses, and attorneys, having left their chairs, were grouped round the map on which a scientific witness was laboriously pointing out the spot to which his evidence related.

In another court in the same building a State judge was dealing out justice on the previous day's offenders against the public peace, and the fairness with which a Chinese thief's defence was heard there contrasted bitterly with the scanty justice honest Chinamen received from their neighbours in the streets and lanes of the city.

Montgomery Street is as crowded as Cheapside in the middle of the day. The mining-brokers and their clients stand thick as bees on the pavements, and a hum as loud as from a hive at swarming-time rises as you pass by.

The edges of the roads are lined with the one-horse buggies of the merchants and business men of all sorts from streets even but a few hundred yards off; and the horses stand half on, half off, the side-walks, each with a leathern halter tied to a four-pound weight, taking no interest in the bargaining which fills the air, but patiently waiting till it pleases his lord and master to finish his business, his luncheon, and his drinks, and mount again.

Close by are several free luncheon-rooms. In the basements generally of buildings full of offices above, are these large rooms, each expensively fitted with polished woods, silver fittings, and marble counters. You enter and pay at the counter on your right twelve and a half or twenty-five cents, according to the notice posted up; then the world of drinks is before you, and any one you ask for is at your service.

Your payment also entitles you to the free run of the counter at the far end of the room, on which stand steaming dishes of soup, clam-chowder, chicken-gumbo,[1] roast turkey with cranberry-sauce, sucking-pig and apple-sauce and all the other dishes of the season. White-jacketed waiters press you to eat, and it is a marvel how you get so much for giving so little. But it pays, as witness the fortunes of the proprietors.

The post-office arrangements differ from ours. Most of the business people have little lockers at the office open to the inside to receive the letters as they arrive, but closed on the side next the public passage by a door with a tiny latchkey, and so free only to the owner for the time being of the key. The letters are fetched at any moment in the twenty-four hours.

The post-office and the custom-house both stand on ground reclaimed from the bay by the cutting down of the rocky hills behind. Five and twenty years ago ships discharged their infrequent cargoes on this very spot, and there were twenty feet of water where now streets run and public offices have been built. Five

---

[1] " Chicken gumbo." More soup than stew, vegetables in plenty, especially small slices of the okra-bean, with a flavour specially its own. Once tasted, always to be taken, if only opportunity offers.

and twenty years seems an indefinite time, but put it
into figures, and say that in 1850 tents and shanties
constituted the city, and the only solid buildings were
the old Spanish mud-built Dolores church and its
surrounding mission, and one can realise the change.

One of our friends made his fortune as a watch-
maker in those early years.   He and one other were the
only men who could replace a broken watch-glass : his
stock was not large.   If a burly miner came in with
his gold dust to have his glass refitted, often our friend
was not able in his scanty store to find the right one.
His dodge was to say, " Just wait while I go into my
shop and grind this smaller"; and out he ran to his
neighbour's shop by a back way to see if he could find
the right one there.   Then returning, he charged three
or four dollars for what now is worth but a few cents,
and readily the price was paid.

Every Sunday in those good old times a main of
cocks was fought close by the old church, and the
churchyard was handy to receive the weekly victims of
the rows which regularly broke out.

Then were the days of the Vigilance Committee,
which alone restrained the passions of those utterly
lawless men ; an organisation which was happily

renewed in this very summer to redeem the city from the power of the mob.

Even yet men go armed about their daily work. As we passed down from the hotel along the street a crowd was gathered round a chemist's shop. Inside a man was breathing his last, shot " on sight " with a revolver by a man with whom some trivial quarrel had arisen from a hasty push on leaving the lift by which both men had descended from their bedrooms to breakfast. But public opinion was against the murderer, and he only escaped by suicide in the prison the doom for which he was surely destined. So the times are past, never to return, when "a man for breakfast " was the regular item in the daily papers.

The Chinese quarter in San Francisco, however, is the sight of the city.

Having arranged, by the courtesy of the chief of police, for the services of a detective whose beat was in this quarter, we left the hotel about eight in the evening. In ten minutes we had reached Dubois Street, and were in the other hemisphere. No other white men but our three selves were in sight; the crowd, jostling, laughing, pushing, was of yellow-faced, pig-tailed, blue-clothed men.

The shops had Chinese signs, exposed for sale only
Chinese goods, the workshops in the basements were
crowded with Chinese workmen, each at his bench,
lighted with a flaring wick burning in a tray of oil;
the restaurants sold tea; hawkers of strange vegetables
and unwholesome-looking meat passed and repassed;
here and there a Chinese woman with baggy black
trousers, curiously braided hair, and jade bracelets on
each arm, carrying a broad-faced, narrow-eyed baby,
made her way through the crowd, and the air was
heavy with novel scents, none of them pleasant to our
nostrils.

We went down the steps from the street into one
of the basement workshops.

Six or seven jewellers were at work.   Each had his
dirty black tray before him, and with long, slender,
dirt-grimed fingers and delicate tools, was nipping off
morsels of gold wire, and beating and twisting and
joining them into filigree work, which contrasted
strangely in its brightness with the dingy, crowded
room, coarse black benches and greasy lamps and dirty
workmen.

The next was a shoemaker's, equally crowded, where
the pointed, wooden-soled, straw-lined shoes were being

made.   Then we went into a druggist's shop and asked
to be served with opium ; the salesman refused, deterred
by the recognition of the police-badge of our companion, it being against the regulations of the city for
Chinese to sell opium to white men.   But trade was
to be done and money made; so outside the shop a
smiling youngster said, "You give me dollar, I buy
opium, you give me one bit."   And so the law was
evaded successfully as ever, where both parties to the
bargain desire so to do.

Then we went into the Chinese theatre.   A good-
sized place, with no money wasted on the wooden
benches, uncoloured walls, flaring gas-burners, and
bare, boarded stage.

It was crammed with a very appreciative audience of
men, and in a side gallery sat, equally intent on the
performance, some six or eight lady members of the
families of the better-off merchants and shopkeepers.

Most of the men wore their hats, and leaned eagerly
forwards on their elbows on the back of the bench in
front, and at every point made by the actors a round of
laughter, different in tone from an English or American
laugh, ran through the theatre.

At the back of the stage sat, in a semicircle, the

orchestra. There were six musicians : in the centre, on a high stool, was the leader, a violinist, dressed in blue silk, with long, hanging sleeves lined with dirty white silk. He carried a blue silk handkerchief up one sleeve, and at every pause he drew it out, flourished it gracefully, and wiped his steaming brows, all with an air that Joachim or Vieuxtemps*might envy. He played on a long-necked, small-bodied, two-stringed instrument, with a bow which worked between the two strings. When a change in the key was wanted he changed violins with the greatest agility, picking out the one he wanted from a row of five or six, arranged on a shelf behind his head.

On his right was a drummer, playing a very small and high-toned drum, and next him was a man having what appeared to be a larger fiddle, which was not changed. On the left of the leader was a banjo-player, whose accompaniment was constantly going. Next him was a player on cymbals ; and, in a recess in the wall behind the violinist, was a fiend with several gongs, which accentuated all the stops in the music, and filled the theatre with a most hideous din.

We had heard that a Chinese play lasted for months, and followed the *dramatis personœ* from cradle to

burial; if so, we chanced on a very exciting, melo-
dramatic period in the lives of the hero and heroine.
Two lovers were kept from happiness by a wicked
mandarin, who employed a bravo with a sword to kill
the gentleman. But the lady's sister was a member of
the mandarin's household, and proceeded to poison him
by putting arsenic in his tea. The mandarin died
peaceably in his chair while his bravoes were dragging
the gentleman lover into his presence to slay him.
Then a fight between the lover and the ruffians, in
which virtue triumphed and wickedness fell reeling on
the ground. But more followers of the mandarin came
to the rescue, and the lovers escaped in a boat with the
heroine's sister, who had poisoned the mandarin, and
with the help of two honest boatmen.

Then the wicked mandarin was carried to his burial,
and we could stand the noise and heat and smell no
longer, and left the farther history of the lovers to be
imagined, not seen.

The actors were all men: their voices, pitched in a
high falsetto recitative, with a sing-song at the end of
a sentence which reminded one strongly of a feeble
attempt at intoning in church at home. The actors
playing female parts had to set their voices still

higher, and at the least excitement they fairly screamed. The acting was full of conventionalities, as was the scene-setting, and also the properties.

If a blow were necessary, it was aimed, but stopped short; the fight with swords was regular one, two, three-work; the boat was indicated by a small piece of carpet on the stage, on to which the escaping lovers leaped, and two long sticks served the boatmen for oars. Death was shown by a white silk banner brought on by two stage assistants, and held in front of the dead man, and burial was set forth by the deceased walking boldly off the stage, followed by the white banner and its bearers. Two or three old chairs and a table, a tea-kettle, and a rusty sword or two formed the scenes and properties.

As we followed what was to us of course the dumb-show of the performance, it was interesting to be made to feel that we were looking, not at the elementary efforts of a half-savage nation, but at the fully-developed, traditional results of play-acting having a history of centuries.

After the theatre to the restaurant in due course. We looked in at one or two; but they were full, and steamy. At each small table were two or three Chinamen, each with a saucerful of shell-fish soup, and a bowl of rice in common. At last we found a place of a superior sort, where a green verandah on the first floor, hung with paper lanterns, looked clean and tempting. Down stairs there was the usual crowd, but up stairs the room looking on to the verandah was empty, except for two opium-smokers at one end, reclining on a raised bench, and leaning on their elbows over the little stove between them holding the fire for their pipes.

An English-speaking waiter was found, who was smoking mild, sweet tobacco in a heavy, brass-mounted pipe. We ordered tea and sweetmeats; he found us stools, which he set round a table, and brought a delicate china teapot and cup for each person. Then he put a good large spoonful of tea into each little teapot, and a lad brought a great brass kettle of boiling water, from which each teapot was filled. Cakes of various colours, made of some sweet-tasting stuff like maccaroons, then came on in a tray. The tea was poured by the waiter from each man's teapot into his cup, and we were left to nibble and sip.

All this while the opium-smokers at the end of the room never turned an eye on us—absorbed, body and soul, in moulding the little pea of opium between finger and thumb, then placing it on the pipe; then, lighting the pipe at the little charcoal stove between them, they took just three whiffs, deliberate and happy, and the pipe was out, and all was to do over again.

They were people above the lowest class; but, after our tea was done, we saw opium-smoking in full blast. Hovel after hovel we entered, in one dark alley after another, to find each filled with the peculiar sickly smell of the smoke, and crowded from floor to ceiling, on broad shelves ranged round and across, like berths on shipboard, with couples of languid, anything but *washed*-out looking wretches—never speaking, only moving to replenish their pipes and re-light them. Other miserable huts were filled with lodgers, all alike crowded: some cooking, some eating, all tea-making; some card-playing, some tobacco-smoking, all talking and laughing together.

Nearly all were men; one or two alleys contained Chinese women of the lowest class, who have lately been brought over in considerable numbers. Then we stumbled up a dark entry, and up two flights of ruinous wooden steps, past three or four crowded lodging-houses, to the Joss House, or temple. But it was closed ; and the priest in charge had gone out visiting ; so we had to content ourselves with seeing the outside of the tumble-down building, the door-posts covered with red characters, lighted by a swinging paper lantern or two.

Up that court was the only place in all Chinatown where we received anything but perfect civility. There the inhabitants were evidently of the roughest order, and seemed disinclined to move to let us pass either in or out. It was pitch dark, and one could not but think how far we were from help should rudeness develop insult or violence.

But we took no notice of any, and passed out unmolested into the streets, by this time silent and dark. One or two Chinese chiffoniers, with basket and lantern, were turning over the heaps of refuse by the doors ; but we watched them for some time without their finding anything worth keeping, even to their unfastidious judgment. And so we found our way back to the hotel, and dismissed our guide, having crowded more sight-seeing into one evening than ever before.

The Chinese labourers are brought over by the Chinese companies, formed by wealthy and responsible men, who contract to hire out their fellow-countrymen, from one to five hundred, for all imaginable trades and purposes. Do you want a cook or valet ? You go to the company : they will find you the servant, and keep you supplied as long as you please : change him as often as you wish : and meanwhile guarantee his fidelity and honesty.

They are a strange people these Chinese house-servants. A friend of ours, as kind and good a master as servants could have, had occasion to discharge a Chinese waiter or footman : after that no one would stop with him. One after another left him after one day in the house, no reason assigned. He changed his company and got a fresh servant from a fresh source ; but it was no use ; he left, and was followed by a succession.

Our friend was at his wits' end. At last he besought an acquaintance who had a Chinese body-servant who was much attached to him and had lived with him for years to bring John to look over the servants' quarters. John and his master came and went over the house from bottom to top. At last John burst out laughing. "What's the matter ?" said his master. "Look here, sah," said the man, pointing to a few scratches on the wall in the servants' bedroom, " say massa Johnson got evil eye : no good stay with him."

And so the matter was explained : a dash of white-wash set matters straight, and obliterated the legacy of trouble the discharged servant had so artfully prepared.

Nearly all the house-servants, gardeners, railway labourers, scavengers, and laundry-men in and round San Francisco are Chinese. No white men can com-pete with them in their own branches in point of cheapness and certainty of work ; and the system of supply and guarantee by the companies does away with the drawbacks of their occasional fickleness, incompetency, and dishonesty.

One master of our acquaintance was robbed by his two Chinese servants of several thousand dollars worth of jewellery and plate. But the company at once made his loss good, though what became of the dishonest servants was never known. Probably they went back to China in coffins, numbers of which, restoring the dead Chinamen to the graves of their ancestors, form a lucrative part of the cargo of many of the steam-ships for Hong-Kong and Shanghai.

But you must not put a Chinaman to have

anything to do with a horse: they are not bred for it: they fear the horse, and seem utterly unable to ride, drive, feed, or harness him. They will learn to manage a steam-engine, but not a horse. There is a record of only one exception ; he was a servant of a friend of ours, and we heard with great admiration that Sam could not only drive, but shoot flying. The effort was too great, however, and Sam lived but a year or two after he had attained this glory.

We were at San Francisco on the 4th of July. Half the city went mad, and the other half looked on at their antics.

For days before the newspapers gave lists of the marshals and deputy-marshals of the day.

The order of the procession was also given ; and about ten in the morning, the shops all being shut, we stood among a most good-natured interested crowd, mostly of women and children, to see the whole string pass. There were the marshals ; at ordinary times douce, respectable heads of families, to-day decked out in cocked hats with feathers, and white gauntlets, and braided frocks and trousers, pacing about on horse-back with rulers in their hands : they showed the way to all the military companies. Horse, foot, and

artillery, all fairly drilled and all well-armed, marched
past. The Germans, French, and Italians, in separate
companies of Grenadiers, Zouaves, and Garibaldini,
with red shirts, made a gallant show.

Then came all the trade societies, with scarves and
banners, marching four abreast.   Their line was
broken by various devices: here a huge waggon of
flourbags decked with garlands was provided by the
bakers; next a waggon with wine casks, and young
girls with full baskets of grapes symbolised the vineyards of the State : then one with a high piled trophy
of pumpkins, carrots, cucumbers, cauliflowers and all
other vegetables, had been arranged by the gardeners;
and so on.

Not the least picturesque part of the show was
made up of the teamsters, each bestriding a huge
but compact drayhorse, with bright new harness
decked with gay ribbons, and all the riders in
uniform of white shirt-sleeves and dark-blue waistcoats and trousers, and new wide-brimmed straw
hats.   After parading the city for some hours the
procession halted at one of the large public halls,
where, as in various other buildings, large audiences
assembled to hear orations from popular speakers on

the memories of the day, the glories of America past, present, and future. The day concluded with a general discharge of fireworks in and about the streets—crackers were exploding everywhere, guns firing, and a general hullabaloo lasted till two or three in the morning before the tired-out revellers got to rest. The next day the uniforms had disappeared, the shops and offices were all open, a double quantity of money-making had to be got through, and nothing but a very jaded, late-to-bed, brandy-and-soda look about most men's faces reminded you of the Glorious Fourth.

Of course there should be an account given of the big trees and of the Yosemite valley. So many pages have however been written about them that we have pity on the reader and pass on—the more readily because there was so little water in the rivers, owing to the drought, that the waterfalls were not worth seeing: so a visit to these wonders of the world is postponed for us till the next time we are passing that way.

Every Californian, however, very early in his talk with you, guesses that you have been up to the Yosemite. You reply, "Well, no, I have not." He always says, "Ah! you should go: must not leave California without seeing them."

We were very kindly made free of the Pacific Club during our stay in San Francisco. The first afternoon, after being introduced to more than a dozen members, we sat in the smoking - room chatting. Every one advised the Yosemite. So we turned on a grey-bearded, impressive colonel, who was giving us very strong exhortations to go at once. "Well, sir, when were you there last?" "Well, sir, I have been intending to go up this very fall." "Have you never been?" "Well, sir, I have always found myself too busy to go there except just for my holiday, and then I have had to go with the family to the sea, or up into the mountains to shoot." And then we questioned each in turn, to find that only one out of six of these natives had ever been there himself.

It is a five days' trip from San Francisco, and not entirely pleasant to some people.

A good many miles of stage up the mountains and down again have to be passed. Large open stages with six horses, like an English break, but with three cross seats, holding three each, in the body of the carriage, are preferred for the summer travelling.

One of our friends was going up to the Yosemite: when he got to Merced station for the stage, he found a fat, white-faced priest was to be one of his companions. This gentleman, being out for a holiday, chaffed this and joked that man, and at last tried to take a rise out of the stage-driver. They had not long started: the six blood-horses were toiling up the first part of the ascent, and had dropped from their run into a walk.

The driver was also owner of the stage and team; a tall, dried-up, powerful Californian, intent on his work, speaking but little except to his horses, and set on getting through his long day's work, but proud of his coach and horses to the backbone. " Well, Mr. Adams," said the priest, "is this all you can do for us ? Not much pace about this travelling: I always thought you gentlemen could drive, and your teams could go." Mr. Adams cast one look over his shoulder from his box seat at the broad grinning face of the padre, who was comfortably seated on the forward cross seat below, nearest therefore to the driver, but he said not a word.

Presently the priest tried again, but failed to get any reply from the grave, sober-looking driver. So they toiled up the mountain. Presently they stopped at a wayside inn, and some country women got in. The stage-driver is absolute master of the loading of his coach, so he handed the ladies in, and signed to the priest to move on to the back seat overhanging the wheels, and the back of the stage altogether. The father grumbled, but went.

Some more folk were picked up on the road and put into their places inside, and the priest was gradually edged into the last outside seat on the right-hand, or off-side.

After an hour or two zigzagging up they reached the top, the priest never ceasing his jokes, and small ones they were.

The horses stopped to breathe, and then paced gently along the level at the top. The view opened out, and they saw the road twisting and turning down the steep grades below them, with a precipice of hundreds of feet down to the river below. They could see miles of this before them, and the road looked but a thread in the straight bit at the bottom.

The passengers shook a little in their places at the prospect, but Mr. Adams remarked, generally, as he handled his "lines," "Not much pace about this travelling, you bet."

The first turn in the grade came, and the tail-end of the long coach swung round vehemently, the wheels skirring and grating on the stones, hard locked. Every one winced, and the priest, having the full benefit of the swing and of the prospect down the mountain side, shrunk away and shut his eyes. Presently Mr. Adams shook up his six bays, and threw his long lash among them with a smack.

The horses bounded as if traces and reins must alike go; and down they skated, stones flying, brakes creaking, wheels striking a chain of sparks, and the heavy coach swaying at each turn in the zigzag, till the off hind-wheel, with the fat priest above it, fairly overhung the precipice below.

The women cried out, the men shivered, the priest let go the side of the coach to clasp his hands, with his eyes turned to the skies, and his white lips muttering rapid prayers to all the saints in his calendar.

Down they went, faster and faster, till the horses

were at a rapid gallop, and the noise and rattle, and
dust and stones flying, nearly drove every one wild.
Mr. Adams sat unmoved, except to ply his brake
with his right foot harder and harder, till the hind-
wheels were absolutely locked, and jumped and skidded
till it seemed as if wood, leather, and iron could
never stand the strain. The priest turned sickly,
ghastly white, expecting each moment to be his last;
but the pace round the turns kept them on the road,
and they gained the bottom safely, a sorely-bruised
and shaken and frightened crew. As the horses
dropped into a gentle trot, Mr. Adams looked back
once again and quietly remarked, "Sometimes we *kin*
get pace on this road."

Having one clear day to spare, we devoted it to
the Geysers. We left San Francisco in the early
morning, went on board the steamer *Donahue*, which
plies between San Francisco and the little town of
Donahue, and crossed the bay.

The white mist was clearing off, and one by one the
islands came in sight. We passed Alkatross Island
with its fort and casemates, where some of the last
political prisoners of the Civil War spent weary
months, while the civil courts debated, and ultimately

reversed, the sentences of the military courts. Then San José*and Vallejo showed us their white houses nestled at the foot of the great brown hills.

The little waves of the bay died away as we passed between flat, broad marshes into a smooth lagoon, and then into a river winding along, with but just room for the steamboat to make her way, the blue water of the bay exchanged for the absolute white of the river on which the low rays of sunlight were dazzling to the eye. Flocks of white gulls were seated in rows on the fences surrounding the scattered cottages of the fishermen, one every now and then dipping into the water after some little fish, and sending circles ever widening, till the steamboat crossed and covered them all.

Then the hills drew nearer to the water's edge, and slopes covered with yellow wheat stubbles, broken here and there with vineyards and fields of Indian corn, came one by one into view.

Then we ran alongside a railway station and wharf, and the steamer, butting her prow into the opposite muddy bank, swung gently round into her place, and all the passengers entered the train in waiting. We steamed gently up the rich valley, passing one or two little towns bathed in sunshine, and reached Cloverdale, the end, at present, of the line,[*] which has been designed and executed, and is, we believe, owned by Mr. Donahue, who has given his name to town and steamboat.

Nothing is more striking in California than the insight and enterprise of some of these successful men, whose names are on every one's tongue. First, carefully weighing the chances of success, they are slow to "take hold" of a project (to use the expressive term in common use there). But being convinced that there is "money in it," nothing stops them; and devoting themselves to the one object, they succeed.

If you ask to whom this great town house, covered with ornament inside and out, or this lovely country-house, with deep green verandah, seated among its oak-trees, with far-stretching views, belongs, the answer is sure to be, to one or other of the Central Pacific founders, or to some other magnate who has planned, made, and owns some railway, port, or town.

At Cloverdale we found ourselves too late to get a return stage from the Geysers if we waited to go up by the stage leaving at three o'clock ; so we hired a pair-horse buggy, and were driven up. The owner of the livery-stables drove us himself, and told us in conversation how he had twice been burned out, and had lost house, stables, horses, and carriages, and had to begin the world again—taking, however, but three or four years in that prosperous place to regain his former possessions.

The mountain road, smooth and well engineered, though dusty, wound through groves of oak and laurel, with bushes of the poison-oak, with bright green and red leaves intermixed, and overhanging the road. The river below, in ordinary years a swift trout-stream, had shrunk, in this summer's drought, into a string of dull green pools. As the pass opened out, and the mountains rose higher on each side, there were several quicksilver mines, high up near their tops, with long tramroads from the mines to the level of road and river below, where the reducing works were placed, and full cars were running down the steep incline, loaded with the deep red ore, dragging upwards by their weight the empty trucks.

We reached the Geysers Hotel, charmingly placed, with a huge oak in the angle of the house, over-

shadowing the rooms on each side. The sulphurous
scent from the Geysers canon opposite filled the air.

After shaking, brushing, and washing off the white
dust which lay thickly on us, we crossed the little
stream in front of the hotel by a rustic bridge, and
passed up into the side of the mountain. It was a
narrow cleft, in which several pools of black water, a
few feet across, were connected by a trickling rill.

The hill-sides were black and red, and then streaked
with yellow, where the imprisoned gases were finding
their exit to the air. The earth shook, and a sound
of rushing and boiling grew louder and louder, as we
climbed higher up into the canon.

Steam rushed from every orifice, and fresh ones
were easily made by thrusting the sticks we carried
through a thin crust of soil. The incrustations of
sulphur formed delicate yellow tracery over the black
mud, and the hill-sides in places were deep red with
cinnabar. Not a blade of grass grew in the cleft,
which looked as if the explosion which had torn the
hill-side asunder and left its ashes smoking everywhere,
had but just burst out.*

A chemist would find a month's work in the com-
pounds of sulphur, iron, and quicksilver before his

eyes. We mounted to the top, and stood on what looked like a huge bubble thrown up in the soft earth. "Jump," said the guide, and the whole excrescence shook and waved till we expected to plunge through into a hot gulf below. "Never fear," said he, "I have been here seventeen years. I weighed only 112 pounds when I came, and now I am sixty-eight and weigh 150 pounds, and I have jumped here most days—so I think it will bear us all, and more too." So sulphur fumes and steamy air sometimes cure; and the guide's experience may give promise for a sulphur-steam cure; who knows?

The night was falling as we drove back, seeing nothing on the road till we passed a great four-horse waggon with iron pots of quicksilver being taken from the mines to the market. We were suddenly startled by two armed men pushing through the bushes into the road; they said they were trying for a shot at a bear. We had our suspicions that their intention was to stop the stage soon expected to pass; however, they let us by. The road was dangerous in the dark, with its sharp turns and steep zigzags, and we were not sorry to get to our comfortable inn at Cloverdale.

The night was pitch dark. We were smoking in the

verandah after supper, and chatting with the landlord,
hearing his adventures as a Union soldier in the war,
when an Indian pony came quietly along the sandy
road and stopped suddenly in the strong light of the
lamp, while its rider, a big, straw-hatted Indian, rolled
off the pony and mysteriously beckoned the landlord
away from us. He followed the Indian into the dark,
and we saw another Indian on his pony holding the
first man's horse. The landlord said loudly, "No, I
tell you; no, not a drop," and returned to us. The
Indians stood sulkily in the edge of the darkness and
we went to bed, the landlord showing us to our rooms
and leaving the down stairs rooms all open and lighted,
with money and drink and property all abroad. "Are
you not afraid," said we, "to leave those Indians there
with everything open?" "What?" he answered,
"afraid of that riff-raff? No, nor twenty like them;
fifteen years ago that Indian would have shot the man
who refused him whisky as I did; but now they are
as tame as sheep." And from our rooms above we
saw them mount and ride off into the black night.

We heard the sad experiences of a young Englishman

This last summer has been a terrible one for the
farmers in the south of the State.

We heard the sad experiences of a young Englishman

who had been out for three years, had sunk his ready
money in the purchase and stocking of a ranch, had
sent for and married a charming little English girl,
but was then making his way back to England to try
and get some more funds to start afresh. He told us
he had 3,000 sheep which he had been glad to sell for
sixpence apiece, as they were starving on the ranch,
and there was neither hay to buy nor money to pay
for it.

His wife's experiences on the ranch, ten miles from a
town, and no lady but her sister-in-law within reach,
were most amusing. She said they got up very early
and turned out on horseback before breakfast to see
after the stock. Then coming in, her husband set the
breakfast things while she cooked the bacon, made the
bread, and ground and made the coffee. After breakfast they gardened, and saw to the orchard of olives and
oranges and almonds till it was time to think about
dinner. Then cooking the dinner amused them a long
while, and the afternoon gave them a siesta. Then as
the cool evening drew on another long gallop all round
brought them in tired to supper ; then a little while for
music and reading and then to bed. " And have you
not got tired of this life ? " we said to the little lady, as

fresh in complexion and neat in toilet as if Brighton
and not Santa Barbara had been her home for two
years past. "Oh dear, no," she said, "Bob is so good ;
he never made wry faces over the messes I used to
make at first, and now I am a good cook, and it was
glorious fun, like pic-nics always ! " and " Bob " looked
on smiling, a great broad-shouldered Englishman,
proud of nothing but his little brave wife.

He confided to us that having no female servants in
the house was " rather a bore," and said they preferred
to cook for themselves rather than let the farm helps
touch the food.

He told us that the want of water on the ranch was
the great drawback ; and that a year and a half ago
his help had persuaded him to let a Spanish water-
finder come to try his skill; that an old wizened, velvet-
jacketed, silver-buttoned Spaniard had come and
marched gravely about the place, had then produced the
familiar forked switch and gone slowly round. That
then a spot at the foot of a hill near the buildings had
been shown as the place where there was water, but not
good. That they had dug there and found a brackish
spring. That the old water-finder had marched off
again with his stick, and presently pointed out the foot

of another hill near by as a place where there was some
water, good but not abundant. That there also his
words had come true, and that they had used that
spring for drinking ever since.

Our friend, with true British pluck, was ready
enough to try his fortune again, and hoped in a year or
two to have ranch and flock and herds; and, above all,
the drove of pigs which was his particular hobby, and
which were to make him the richest of rancheros in
the shortest time.

When we returned to San Francisco we dined with
the owner of one of the largest vineyards in Napa
county in the State. We heard of the patient efforts
by varying the kinds of grapes and getting over vine-
dressers from Champagne, Burgundy, and the Rhine
country, which have now been made for years past to
get a wine worthy of the soil and climate.

The San Franciscans know exceedingly well what
good wine is, and they import some of the best; our
observation was that they were much more anxious that
the British stranger should taste their native wine than
to drink it themselves. We agree with them quite.
Taking a gentle sip of Californian Burgundy, roll it

round your tongue and swallow it slowly—say, "Ah, this is really good!—the true Burgundy flavour!"— then *fill* your other glass with the genuine Pomard, and say, "But this is perhaps more mature!" and drink it all. Your friend will be pleased that you admire his native wine, and drink his French wine—and he will ask you to dinner again.

And what hospitable people they are! You go to a friend's house to dine, and sit next a chatty, pleasant fellow—he says, "What are you going to do in the morning? Come down with me to the Cliff House to breakfast, and then I want you to meet some of our scientists, so come and dine at six, and I will get one or two of our professors to come in; and next week one or two of us are going up to our little place in the mountains to shoot, and you must come and kill a deer and a bear, and there are lots of duck and quail." This kind of thing is repeated, until the English stranger thinks with remorse of the American friends who have come over to England with introductions to him, and whom he has dismissed with a dinner at the club, and a sense that he has then performed towards them the whole duty of man. The fact is that the Americans are a more friendly people then we, visit each other more freely and with less ceremony by far, habitually having one night in the week open for their acquaintances to come and share in the talk, music, dancing, or cards, which are going on.

CHAPTER IV.

AFTER a few more days in San Francisco we prepared
for our intended journey overland to Oregon. And it
is a serious matter to go in for two days and three
nights in a stage, when one knows what a stage is, and
what the roads are. To pass night after night, either
on a high box-seat with a low back, where you dare
not do more than doze lightly for fear of falling off, or
in the inside, which is worse. Three seats, and room
for three passengers on each ; two seats facing each
other as usual at the front and back of the carriage,
and the third across, just behind the doors, with a
broad leather strap for the only back. On two out of
the three seats your head strikes against the wooden
supports of the leather sides and top of the coach
the moment you "drop off," and on the middle seat
your head, having no support, seems to be always
dropping off you. Then every one has at least four

legs inside, for you can never find a quiet space for yours; and, again, just as you can hold up no longer, and sleep is stealing over you, creak, gur-r-r, crack go the hind wheels just under you, as the brake comes violently into play down hill, and the stones fly. And the dust!

And in the little eating-houses—inns you cannot call them—where the stage stops for meals, you are fed chiefly on small, square bits of tough, fried meat, with fried potatoes, and sometimes pie. (This last you would eat of more freely were it not for the legions of house-flies, which dispute with you every mouthful!) As we heard of all these things, and of the dangers of the road, from accidents to the stage, and robbery of the stage and all its passengers, we were half inclined to go by sea from San Francisco to Portland, and fight shy of the stage. But we stuck to the road, which now has to be described.

Instead of going to Sacramento by rail on our way north to Redding, we determined on leaving by the Vallejo boat, and then the rail along the Sacramento river valley. All our friends came to see us off, after the fashion in those parts. The

Americans laugh at their own fondness for leave-taking, and certainly it is carried to an absurd extreme.

What American writer is it who tells the story of how he went down by boat south, and as he stood on deck alone, in the middle of a crowd of passengers waving handkerchiefs and shouting fare-wells, he felt lonely, and thought he would like some one to say farewell to him too? So he sung out, "Good-bye, Jack — good-bye;" and a voice replied, "Good-bye, old fellow; a pleasant journey to you." But one was not enough, so he cried, "Good-bye, Captain—good-bye;" and three hats were swung, and three answers came. "Good-bye, *Colonel* — good-bye," the traveller cried. Fifteen handkerchiefs were waved as the vessel moved off. "Good-bye, GENERAL—good-bye," was the traveller's last shout; and a chorus of voices returned his greeting, and a grove of handkerchiefs and a swarm of hats were shaken till the figures grew smaller and smaller, and their voices still crying "Good-bye, old fellow—good-bye," faded away.

Vallejo has an older look than most of the Cali-fornian towns, and is as pleasantly situated on the

bay as San Francisco herself: the navy yard of
Mare Island is close by, the chief repairing yard for
the United States navy on the Pacific coast. At
Vallejo we took the train up the valley, and reached
Sacramento at half-past eleven having left at seven,
instead of leaving at eight and arriving at three, by
the usual route, *viâ* Oakland.

We went on north at half-past three, and until
midnight, when we reached Redding, we were passing
through a lovely valley, well wooded with fine oak
trees, and occasional thickets of laurel and cotton
woods by the streams.

At Redding, where is the terminus at present of
the Californian and Oregon railroad, we found the
stage in waiting. The talk, half-joke and half-
earnest, was as to hiding or not hiding our money.
We all knew that there was a chance of being
stopped and robbed; but, till we mounted the stage,
we did not know that it had been stopped five
times in the last eighteen months, or we should
have been more inclined to take the advice of
friends, who insisted that the only safe place for
our money was in our socks.

By one o'clock at night we started, the luggage-rest

at the back being piled with luggage and post-bags, and on the top being fastened a heavy, strong box of Wells, Fargo, and Co.'s, for money and valuables. The four horses had quite enough to do to drag the stage up the first hill, laden as it was inside and out.

We had the advantage of the box-seat next Charlie McConnell, the prince of drivers. He handled his horses, and worked the heavy brake, and smoked cigars, and chatted unceasingly to his two box-seat passengers, doing all equally well.

The night was dark, but clear, the stars shining; but in the woody glades we soon entered we were glad enough of the strong light thrown down the road by the large bright lamp fixed under the splash-board over the pole.

We crossed first a bare heathy ground, strewn with rocks, then entered a wood, the road descending rapidly. "Look out for yourselves at the bottom, gentlemen," said McConnell. "If we are going to be stopped on this stage, there will be the place," pointing to a level ending in a sharp rise upwards, and having a clear space of thirty yards or so before the wood began. "They always choose a place where one can stop the horses when they are at a walk ; and the other, fifteen or twenty yards off, covers the driver and outsides with a double gun, loaded with buckshot. Don't shoot, gentlemen, unless you are sure of both rascals at once, or we shall all be riddled," he went on, seeing a move to get revolvers ready. "Better lose a few dollars, than risk a charge of buckshot among us."

We passed safely the debateable ground, and shortly the road brought us to the edge of a river, the McLeod,* looking inky black between its tree-covered banks. The ferryman was in waiting, and the horses marched gravely on to the boat, and waited for the crossing. When the coach was settled on the boat, the ferryman turned vigorously a large wheel at the side of the boat, round which a rope was wound, which reached up to a wire-rope stretched high from tree to tree across the stream.

"Seen a fellow on a little black mare pass yesterday or to-day, Jack ?" said McConnell. "No," was the answer. When we got across, McConnell said, "That scamp I asked after, stopped the stage on the other road three days ago; and from the description, he is the same fellow who robbed us last

November, and took my watch. He is in this
country, and can only get out by one of two roads,
and the sheriff is after him. If I hear of him, I
shall go after him myself. The rogue took my
watch—took the driver's watch!" said he, evidently
considering that to rob the stage driver as well as
the passengers was breaking the rules of the game.

Presently he said, "There are two fellows in the
State prison yet, who were taken by one man a year
or two ago." "Tell us about it," we said. "Well,"
he answered, "the stage was going along all right
when a fellow ran to the horses' heads, and two others
covered the driver with their guns in the regular way.
He told the driver to drop the reins, and made the
passengers throw up their hands. Then he told the
passengers to get down and stand in a row by the
roadside, and made the driver throw down the Wells
Fargo box, which was what they were after.

"Then they robbed the passengers all comfortable.
When they came to one man, he asked them to give
him back his watch, which was of no great account
to them, but had belonged to his grandfather. Instead
of being civil, the rascal up with his hand and gave
him a great smack on the face, and told him to hold

his tongue. So they took his watch, and the rest of the watches, and all their money, and then told them to get up again and be off. So they all mounted again, and drove off glad enough to be free.

"As soon as they had gone about a quarter of a mile, or so, the passenger told the driver to stop. 'What for?' says he. 'I am not going to have my face slapped for nothing,' says the passenger. So he got out of the luggage a nice little repeating Henry rifle, and got down off the coach and back he went.

"Presently he saw, as he expected, a light in the bushes near the road. So he crept up through the trees, and saw the three rascals all round the Wells Fargo box, which they were trying to break open; they had put their guns down, never dreaming of danger. The passenger got up within a safe distance till he could cover them well; then he let fly, and the first shot dropped one of them dead, the next winged one of the others, and the third screamed out for mercy. So he went up and made the unhurt one help his wounded fellow back into the road, and then he drove them in front of him till he came up to the coach, and took the two nicely. And they are both in the State prison now," said McConnell.

" When the driver asked the man why he did such a risky thing as go back alone after three, all he said was, 'I was not going to have my face slapped for nothing.'"

And with many tales like this he lightened our way till day broke, and showed us the wood-covered hills and deep valleys we were passing, and the distant mountains on ahead. We drove by the side of the McLeod, where in the pools the salmon were leaping every here and there; the river rushing over rocks, and flashing in the bright morning sun in the rapids and stickles, till we longed to try our luck with salmon fly or phantom.

But it is the rarest thing for these fish, even when fresh run, to take a bait. We heard from a traveller afterwards that he had stopped for three weeks and only caught two fish, one a three-pound grilse, with a spoon bait, and the other a ten-pound salmon, with a bunch of worms. He told us that the trout took the fly pretty freely in the mornings and evenings, and we had a dish of pound or pound and a half fish for dinner, which were part of his spoils.

Soon we came to the government fish-hatching establishment, where there were two or three little

houses for the men employed, and the usual set of
troughs and runs.   We saw several Indians about
who get their living on the river; but they net the
fish, or spear them by torchlight.

Following the stream up, we got to our breakfast
stopping-place, and were introduced to the first of
the fly-filled rooms and dirty tablecloths, and fried
meat, and heavy hot bread, and unwholesome-looking
pies, all of which we were to become so familiar with
during the next day or two.

And then the sun grew hotter, and the dust to rise
in clouds, and we left off one by one our outer garments, and donned the dust-coats of thin alpaca, the
relics of our railway journey across the plains.   The
oaks left us, and we entered the pine region, the trees
only of an average Scotch fir size, and growing sparsely
on the thin stony soil.

We saw a snake or two, which had been basking
in the hot sun, move slowly away before the horses
reached them; the blue jays kept us company all day,
flitting from tree to tree ; but we saw no game birds
or animals, and only a few gophers and squirrels.   As
the day wore on we parted, with regret, from Charlie
McConnell, and did not at all profit by the exchange,

for our new driver shone neither as a whip nor as a companion.

About three o'clock, we stopped by a charmingly-placed little hotel, called Soda Springs,* and on the low wall next the road was placed for us a great jug of the water from which the place takes its name, a natural seltzer water, full of life and effervescence, cool and refreshing. What nectar it was to all of us, dusty and dry! The hotel is a long one-storied white building of wood, with a deep green verandah in two stories, into which both ground floor and first floor rooms opened; and in its shade, in rocking chairs, dressed in light summery costumes, were three or four young ladies and gentlemen. The stern danger of forfeiting our places if we stopped, and being probably delayed for a day or two alone, drove us on, and most unwillingly we climbed to our places and toiled on.

The pine-trees got larger as we mounted, and soon specimens of from three to four feet diameter became not rare. We soon got a sight of the snow-covered, double-headed top of Mount Shasta, and had to take a long half-circle round its base.

This was the first which we had seen of the great volcanic cones, which stretch northwards like sentinels,

guarding the continent from western winds, from
Shasta to Mount Nelson.   All snow-covered, they
catch the earliest and latest sun-rays, and tower, each
in his solitary grandeur, thousands of feet above the
great chain of which they are the ornaments.   Separated by breaks of from fifty to one hundred miles from
each other, yet the air is so clear, and they stand out
so gloriously against the sky, that often three of them
are in sight at once as we travel northwards; and their
beauty consoles us for the gradual lowering of the rest
of the chain, which sink from the crowded broken
mountain-tops of the Sierra Nevada, into the more
uniform shapes and much gentler slopes of the
Cascades.

Late in the evening we stopped to change horses at a
little creeper-covered house, with a few cleared fields,
and some scattered fruit-trees.   The white jessamine
and honeysuckle had spread freely over the porch and
mounted to the roof, and the little grass-plat, next the
road, was planted with rose-trees, which were covered
with flowers.   Our driver lived here, and as the stage
drew near, his young wife and little child stood by the
fence to greet him.

We walked on a little way up the road to get a view

H

through the pines, and came to a clearing where men had felled the trees, and were splitting the logs for planks and shingles. The echo of their tools was the only sound to disturb us as we looked across a patch of fern, and between the red pine trunks to where the mountain shone out crimson before our eyes. One great mass, split near the top into two—with no others near to rival him and dwarf his size—his bare rocky sides of a dull red, with glaciers falling from the snow-cap, showing blood colour below, and vermilion in the full light of the evening sun. We stood entranced, and were repaid in a moment for the heat, dust, rattle, and sleeplessness of the day.

On this higher level the woods were gradually left behind, and we entered long stretches of level land, broken up into farms, with snake fences again lining the road, crops just ripening for harvest, cattle standing belly-deep in rich pasture through which rills of water ran.

The foot-hills of the mountains rose in isolated round buttes—one was the scene of an Indian fight, where among the scrub the band of redskins held their white enemies for long at bay, until ammunition and water failed, and they were massacred to a man.

Then we passed through long thickets of laurel and a sandy tract, where individual firs stood out over the scrub, like specimen conifers in the laurel plantation of a park at home. And then when night had come we reached the mining town of Yreka; the stage stopped for supper, and we exchanged the cool night air, and the continuous soft grinding of the wheels over the sandy road, and the gentle clanking of the harness, for the dazzle of a street lighted from the open doors and windows of five or six saloons, and thronged with miners, who crowded round us as we got down.

After a welcome cup of tea we started again, and dozed on uneasily inside the stage, as it swung down a rapid zigzag descent of many hundreds of feet, the brake hard on all the time, and the hind wheels bumping and jumping from stone to stone.

When morning dawned we were in Oregon, having mounted again in the early hours. A different land-scape greeted us. We were passing between thick woods with close undergrowth of fern, trailing creepers of the wild cucumber, and berry-bearing bushes, black and red.

There was no trace of the stony arid soil of the Californian mountains, with their prevailing tints of

grey, yellow, and light brickdust-red; but fresh green
everywhere round us.   A trickling stream by the roadside had formed a carpet of bright spongy moss,
and the plants of the English woods and hedges, or
their American cousins, seemed like old friends.

We stopped to breakfast at a roadside inn, and were
fed with abundance of cream and wild strawberries.
A clear running rill of water had been led through a
pipe from the hill-side above, and flowed freely through
the tank, where we washed off the dust of our second
night's ride.   We climbed to our places, and started
refreshed for our day's journey.

We passed through a wide tract of undulating
country, green everywhere with woods and copses; on
the upper ranges of the hills the firs showed black in
the distance; but there were wide slopes of corn-land
and grass-fields ripening into their summer yellow, and
here and there a farmer's house, each with its wide
verandah, and fruit-trees round it, with its one barn
and stable.   The corners and angles of cleared land,
cutting into the woods above, showed that the settlers
were extending their cultivated fields and developing
the productiveness of the country; and the soil, red or
dark grey in prevailing tints, and free from rock and

stone, prepared us, on the very boundary of the State, for the fertility we were to take note of for hundreds of miles on our northward journey.

As the day wore on the heat became oppressive, while the sun poured down on the road, winding through the valleys. We passed one or two little towns and villages, all looking prosperous, with new houses being built or old ones enlarged.*

By the middle of the day we reached Jacksonville, a town of from 1,000 to 1,500 inhabitants, depending not only on the agricultural riches of the surrounding country, but on the gold mines on the head waters of the Rogue river, which we were soon to pass.

The day being Sunday the town was in absolute quiet; had we been in Scotland there could not have been a more perfect rest from all worldly pursuits. On the road as we drew near the town we passed waggons full of the country people on their way to church or chapel: the women in light print dresses, holding great blue or green umbrellas to protect themselves from the burning sun; the men in dark cloth jackets and trousers and soft felt hats. As the stage approaches they speak to their horses and draw

slowly to the side of the road to let us pass, using
no whip, and scarcely needing to touch the reins to
get instant obedience. So far as horses are concerned, no Humane Society seems wanted in Oregon;
we hardly ever saw one struck, never one maltreated
or overdriven, from one end of the State to the other.

The inside places of the stage were now filled up
close. A farmer's wife, some fifty years of age,
dressed in a brown alpaca suit of gown and tippet,
of a fashion of fifty years back, with brass-rimmed
spectacles on her nose, and tight little curls round
her face, was put in. Her maiden niece, who had
never smiled in her life, and never would, accompanied her, and sat in the corner, stiff, gaunt, and
angular. Then there was a cheery little Jewish bag-
man, who sold sewing-machines all about the country,
and boasted he had left twelve behind him in Jacksonville, and should never see them again; and then
a seller of a new reaping-machine, the wonder of the
century, completed the full number. The farmer's
wife never forgot it was Sunday, and tried to repress
the irrepressible Jew; but he made jokes and told
stories all the more. The reaping-machine man gloried
in having an Englishman to talk to who knew nothing

of reaping machines; so on he droned, explaining
principles and patents, and showing how his machine
could cut and bind into sheaves, while others could
only cut, and so on, till his auditor wished his machine
and him together in the bottom of the Rogue river.

Then we came to the mining district—nearly all
washed out now—only a few Chinamen, picking up
the white men's crumbs, being left. The deposits had
been found generally in the beds of the rivers; so
they had been diverted into fresh channels, and sluices
run; and now the abandoned watercourses, with heaps
of rough stones and gravel, and holes dug here and
there, looked forlorn and ragged beyond description in
the bright, hot sun. The forest was all round us; the
stumps and roots of the trees had not been cleared
from the road, and the horses often ran neatly on
each side of a stump over which the bottom of the
stage passed with only an inch or two to spare.

By this time we had reached the high, rocky, broken
ground dividing the head-waters of the Rogue and
Umpqua rivers, and in the evening came to the little
town of Galesville,[*] where we changed drivers for the
last time.

We were again in the heart of the mountains

surrounding the head of the Rogue river valley.* The
land in the valley was rich and the crops luxuriant,
only the corn which the settlers raise beyond their own
needs they must give to the hogs, for there is no way
of getting it to a profitable market. The stage passing
daily each way with mails and passengers is their one
link to the outer world; but it takes no passengers to
the valley, nor brings any away; summer by summer,
winter by winter, they live on in their isolation, without
even the ordinary farmers' topics of markets, labour,
and stock: self-contained and happy in their freedom
from all wants they cannot supply and from all
ambitions they cannot satisfy.

It reminded one of the Happy Valley of *Rasselas.*
Bounded on all sides by the rugged mountains, the
only road being the rough track by which we were
passing; down the centre ran the river, the only object
reminding one that there was ever haste in this world:
for the ripples and stickles showed that the water was
hurrying to the sea. Green fields of grass and bits of
oats of still brighter green occupied the few hundred
acres of level land by the stream. The white farm-
houses, roofed with grey shingles, were dotted about
(not grouped into villages or hamlets), each with its

orchard and patch of paddock, while here and there
a great chestnut-tree threw a broad patch of shadow
over roof and buildings.

The cattle lay about in the shade or stood
ruminating in the rich grass; and a sense of quiet and
laziness, as of a perpetual Sunday afternoon, filled
the air. No mill had been built to set even the
stream to work; we passed no inn or shop or forge;
we saw no centre of life and action round which the
men would gather either in work or play

Dragging the coach through a river over which
there was no bridge, and then painfully climbing
round a rocky ledge, where the narrow road was cut
bodily out of the rock, and where the tripping of
but one of the six horses must have overthrown the
rest, and rolled us all into the valley a hundred or
two feet below, the team pulled us slowly to the top
of the pass, and we soon were ready to begin the
descent of the last of our many "grades" into the
head of the great Willamette valley.

The night was clear, calm, and cool. The road
ran through thick woods again, with an undergrowth
of tall fern. Four deer, at intervals during the
night, were startled from their feeding by the noise

of our approach, but, dazzled apparently by the bright light from the great lamp in front of the coach, let us get quite close before they sprang hastily off the road, and hurried away into the dark wood.

This last driver was a fit finisher of the drive begun by McConnell so many hours before. Tall, strong, ready, and active, he needed all his powers to keep his team of six travelling safely down this precipitous canon; and the working of the brake by his right foot was so continuous and laborious, that we were not surprised to hear him say to the man seated on the roof behind him—"Please push your knee hard, sir, hard, into the small of my back."

We started down and were glad enough to get safely to the foot, for one needed constantly to repeat to oneself that these men drove this coach daily over this road without accident; and it seemed impossible that some portion of the stage or harness should not give way under the succession of violent strains.

We looked from the stage window, right over the tops of the trees growing on the next turn of the zigzag below. The light from the great lamp in front shone fitfully on the rocks and trees as we rattled past, and

after two hours of this sort of travelling we left the
mountains behind.   The day broke as we were once
more traversing a farming country, and homesteads,
cornfields, and orchards met our eyes.   Somersetshire
was the county in England which the general aspect of
the land recalled to us, with its long stretches of hill
land, its combes and glens, its fertile fields, frequent
apple orchards, and snug homesteads.

And so we passed through a good many miles, till the
little town of Roseburg came into view, its white
houses and church steeple shining in the bright morning sun.   The stage pulled up at the inn before driving
on to the post-office to deliver over the mailbags,
and we got down to stretch and shake our stiff and
weary limbs.

To look back on the journey seemed to pass in
review weeks of travelling, and hundreds of miles of
distance.   One would have thought no less of distance or time could have accounted for such aching
bones, tired heads, bloodshot eyes, and travel-stained
garments.

The journey from California into Oregon was accom-
plished, and we had safely arrived in the land we had
come so far to see. *

CHAPTER V.

To make this record of travel of use to the ordinary reader, who merely looks to add to his knowledge of the far-off parts of the world, and especially to any debating in their own minds what country they should choose for their future residence, it is necessary to give some general description of Oregon.

If the writer appears to express in too strong terms his admiration of the State, he can only plead that he believes that any other visitor, who travelled with mind open to conviction, would feel constrained to sustain his words—and he appeals to facts as to climate, soil, and productions for confirmation.

Oregon, then, is the most north-westerly State in the Union, and lies between the forty-second and forty-sixth degrees of north latitude : nearly corresponding with the South of France and North of Spain. It is bounded on the east by Idaho, on the

west by the Pacific Ocean, on the north by the
Columbia River, and on the south by California and
Nevada.   It extends, on an average, for 350 miles
east and west, and for 275 miles north and south,
and contains 95,274 square miles,* or about sixty
millions of acres.

It is naturally divided into three great districts,
varying in climate, soil, and general conditions.

Western Oregon lies between the Pacific Ocean and
the Cascade Mountains, thus taking in territory of
250 miles from north to south, and about 100 miles
from west to east.   It contains the Willamette Valley,
named after the great river which runs through it
from south to north, falling into the Columbia river
just below the city of Portland.

This valley is about 150 miles in length, and from
thirty to sixty miles in breadth, and contains about
five millions of acres of some of the richest land in
the world.   Only about one-tenth is as yet under
cultivation, the residue is covered with natural grasses,
or with forest and wood and copse.

It is watered not only by the Willamette, but by
numerous tributary rivers and streams; while clear
springs and rills abound on every hill-side.

The valley is not of a uniform dead level, but is broken into by many spurs of low hills, running into it from the Coast mountains on the west, and from the Cascades on the east, while it is dominated at irregular distances by the snow-capped volcanic cones of the Cascades, named The Three Sisters, Diamond Peak, Pitt,* Scott, Thielson, Jefferson, and Hood. This last rises to the height of upwards of 11,000 feet, and, lying nearly due east of Portland, shows to the city his snow-crowned pyramid, misty in the early morning, clear and cool at noonday, and rosy red as he catches the last rays of the western sun.

The coast ranges on the western side of the valley do not rise higher than 4,000 to 5,000 feet in their tallest heads, and the intervals between lie only about 2,000 above the level of the ocean; whilst there are several passes, notably that to Yaquina Bay, hereafter to be described, where only a height of 600 feet has to be passed between the valley and the Pacific.

Down this great valley the tide of population flowed, and Roseburg, Eugene City, Corvallis, Albany, Salem, Oregon City, and Portland are successively passed on our journey northwards through the State. The same route is followed by the railway along the eastern bank of the river, and another line is in progress on the western side; while still another railroad, from Corvallis to the ocean at Yaquina Bay, is in course of construction, and will afford a quicker and easier outlet from the lower and middle parts of the great valley to the coast.*

Wheat grows luxuriantly everywhere; and being both heavy in yield and first-rate in quality, is the farmers' mainstay. With mere scratching of the ground and no care, it yields from twelve to twenty bushels to the acre; but with ploughing of from five to eight inches in depth, and a little attention to keeping down the weeds, but with no manure, from thirty-five to fifty bushels to the acre is obtained. The Oregon wheat is well known, and commands the highest price in the Liverpool market, which in 1876 received four millions of bushels from this source, and it was estimated that in 1877 seven millions of bushels would be exported.

A very good farmer, who owns a beautiful farm of 500 acres on the western foot-hills, about five miles from Corvallis, told us that his crop cost him just ten dollars per acre to prepare for, harvest, and deliver, and his return averaged nearly thirty bushels to the acre, which brought him seventy cents per bushel, or twenty-one dollars in the whole.

We heard and saw evidence of many similar instances of success, which in this land, never ravaged by drought, or laid waste by floods, or swept by tempests, the farmers everywhere expect.

Not satisfied with the bountiful return of nature for the slight labour of once ploughing and then putting in the seed, the Oregon farmer trusts entirely to nature, in many cases for a second and even a third crop. If he has got thirty bushels an acre from the crop he worked for, he relies on about twenty bushels for the next, appropriately called " volunteer ; " and if he still trusts to Providence, he expects about twelve to fifteen bushels in the following harvest. But nature takes her revenge by providing the careless husbandman with an abundant crop of weeds, which, covering the land, enforce double ploughing and absolute rest in the fourth year.

The quantity of wheat ripening for harvest seemed on many farms we saw quite disproportionate to the number of hands available for farming operations. We found, however, that there was in full operation a system of "farming made easy," which explained matters.

There is a class of contractors each owning a large number of horses and the best available machinery, and employing several hands.

Such a man comes to farmer A, and says, "How many acres of wheat do you want put in?" He asks farmers B and C and D the same question, until he has secured a season's work; he then sends, say, six "gang-ploughs," with four ploughshares, and six horses each, and sets to work. By this means he gets through as much work as a steam-plough here, and cultivates a whole stretch of country. After he has finished his last ploughing and sowing, at the end of April, he takes a rest till August (unless a contract for grubbing wood strikes him as advantageous meanwhile). In August he makes similar terms for the harvesting and sacking of the grain, and you may see a great field alive with "reapers," or "headers," and horses and men. Almost as soon as the corn is cut the thrashing-machine is at work, and the wheat is put into sacks and carted off to the river or railroad, on its way to the warehouse.

Thus an Oregon farmer can calculate to a nicety his expenses; and it will not be found far wrong if we say that, counting interest on the purchase-money

I

of his land at twelve per cent. per annum, and his own labour at a dollar and a half, or 6s. a day, and putting in all the expense of ploughing, sowing, harvesting, and storing his corn, the farmer will find the cost of his wheat to be about forty-nine cents, or 2s. 0½d. a bushel; while the average selling price for the last four years has been about seventy-five cents, or 3s. 1½d. a bushel, leaving him with a profit of twenty-six cents, or 1s. 1d. a bushel.

Oats, also, prosper well. The straw often reaches five feet in height, carrying a bright, full head; the standard weight in Oregon is thirty-six pounds to the bushel, but forty-five and even fifty pounds is often reached, with a return of from fifty to eighty bushels to the acre.

No failure of the wheat crop has ever occurred since the settlement of the country, that is, during a continuous period of thirty-three years.

Barns and sheds for keeping the grain are not needed. Thrashing goes on in the fields, and thence the corn is sent directly to the warehouses for use or exportation. "The Oregon exhibition of cereals was one of the most successful at the Centennial Exhibition at Philadelphia. Medals and diplomas were awarded for fifteen varieties of wheat, five of oats, and for white rye in grain, with straw nine feet high; also for 'ninety-day white wheat,' grain and sheaf raised upon land neither ploughed nor harrowed, and yielding thirty bushels to the acre."—Statement published by the State.

Flax, hops, and potatoes are most successfully cultivated, the latter yielding from 150 to 300 bushels to the acre, and the Colorado beetle is as yet unknown.

The ordinary kinds of fruit thrive luxuriantly. Apples, pears, plums, cherries, gooseberries, currants, strawberries, grow in abundance, and of first-rate quality. We saw the apple-trees on the foot-hills laden with fruit, and the farmers told us they were giving apples to the pigs, having no market even for the finest sorts. The owner of a splendid orchard of twelve acres near Corvallis told us he was thinking of cutting down his trees and ploughing his orchard for wheat, not knowing what to do with his fruit.

The woods are full of wild berries: thimble-berries, bright scarlet, with a sub-acid wild flavour; salmon-berries, yellow and sweet; elderberries, black and red; blackberries, like our English fruit; huckleberries, scarlet and shining, and slightly acid in taste, and a large wild strawberry, grow everywhere. Wild cucumber vines, the spiny, egg-shaped fruit of which is relished by the cattle, trail from bush to bush.

A strong growth of oak and cherry and maple-copse is spreading rapidly over the country where cultivation has not yet reached ; the result of the discontinuance of the forest fires, which were set going annually by the Indians before they were transferred to, and limited in, their reservations during the last ten or twelve years.

In many places we watched the operation of clearing going on. The farmer cut a broad path through the scrub with his axe, the young trees and bushes, fifteen or twenty feet in height, being severed from their roots, but inclined over their growing neighbours : turning round a square of half an acre or so in extent, he left the cut wood to dry for a month or six weeks in the summer sun. Then setting fire to the withered boughs and leaves, the fire spread through the living copse inclosed, and a bare, black spot of earth remained, littered with the partly-burned stems and roots. Then a team

of oxen, dragging a heavy plough, was set to work;
and another team, with a strong chain with large
iron hooks attached, dragged out the burned and
charred stumps. These being heaped together, were
again set on fire, and then the ashes scattered over
the land.

Next spring the wheat will be sown, and the land,
reclaimed finally from waste, will become cultivable
ground, returning in the first year's crop the expense
of the clearing.

The foot-hills of the Coast and Cascade ranges are
covered naturally with a luxuriant growth of brake-
fern. We asked several farmers if they did not find
this very hard to extirpate: they replied that all
they had to do was to mow this fern, and scatter
timothy grass-seed, the staple grass of the State,
among the roots. In the very next summer the
grass would overcome and oust the fern, and cattle
would live and fatten the year round on these
slopes.

Throughout this whole great valley, to the top of
the foot-hills of the Cascades, hardly a stone was to
be seen. The roads, indeed, suffered from their
absence; as, having no bottom of solid stone, they

were no better than wide tracks, beaten smooth,
taken from the adjoining soil; in winter, by all
accounts, reduced by the abundant rain to mud; in
summer, lying thick in grey dust. The hills in the
Coast range were covered with rich, strong soil to
their very summits, giving a very civilised look
to the whole country; wherever cleared of scrub,
they afford pasturage to cattle; and wherever level
enough to plough, fine crops of wheat or oats are
raised.

From this great Willamette valley runs, at right
angles from the town of Corvallis, to the ocean at
Yaquina Bay, a wide, broken gap through the Coast
range of mountains.

The Mary river, a tributary of the Willamette,
shows half the way through, and then, after passing
a broad saddle some three miles wide and seven
hundred feet above sea-level, the Yaquina river
rises and flows gently down to the bay.

This whole tract of country is contorted and
broken: steep, green hills, varying from 600 to 1,000
feet in height, or thereabouts, inclose soft, grassy
valleys; and where the little streams run through
the bottoms, the beavers have often thrown their

dams across. Years passing by have shed into these swamps each autumn's shower of leaves, until a deep layer of black vegetable mould has been deposited of unsurpassable fertility.

Where no man has yet claimed these beaver dam "slews" (sloughs?), the swamp-cabbage and a thick growth of succulent rushes cover the ground; while bears and deer haunt these level bits, lying deep in the shadow of the woods. Where grain has been planted, after a way has been cut by the settlers through the ancient dam to drain the land, most abundant crops grow unmanured year by year.

As the soft winds of the coast and the heavy dews temper and moisten the air, a marked change in the vegetation is seen; the fern grows higher, and has to force its way to the light through an undergrowth of "sal-lal," a large kind of whortleberry, with leaves more than double, and fruit nearly twice as large, as those we were familiar with in Norway, Scotland, and Devonshire. Syringa bushes grew vigorously by the wayside. Red and black elder bushes, covered with fruit just turning colour, flourished side by side with a plant called the arrow bush, with a feathery white flower like the deutschia.

It did not need a very strong spirit of prophecy
to foresee a not distant future, when a farm-house
would overlook each of these fertile glens, and herds
of cows would range these now silent hill-sides; when
the saeter-girls of Norway, the Highland lassies with
snood and plaid, and those Swiss maidens from
whom we have begged a draught of milk at the
last summer *chalets* before we breasted the real
work of the Alpine climb, could each and all find
homes, round which their cattle would graze in peace
all the year round, and a heavier yield of butter
and cheese would each year be sent from these
cool hills to the hot and dry mining towns and
manufacturing cities of California.

The Pacific coast of Oregon is indented with bays,
on each of which a settlement has been formed,
and which are rival claimants for selection and
improvement, as a harbour of refuge, by the United
States government.

Between the Californian boundary on the south
and the Columbia river on the north are passed
Ellensburg,* at the mouth of the Rogue river; Port
Orford, under the shelter of Cape Blanco; Empire City, on Coos Bay, with coal-mines recently

developed and yielding well; Gardner, at the mouth
of the Umpqua river; Newport, on Yaquina Bay;
Garibaldi, on Tillamook Bay; and last, but not least,
Astoria, at the mouth of the great Columbia, just
within the bar.

Each of these little settlements has a character of
its own, and each believes that Portland is nothing
to the city which is in course of formation; though,
in fact, the unbiased visitor notices in each, save
in Astoria, and at Newport, in Yaquina Bay, the
drawbacks of narrow, or shallow, or unsheltered
harbours, and the rugged or lofty mountains closing
out the harbour and its circumscribed district from
the great country behind.

The next division of the State may be called Mid
Oregon, and extends from the summit of the Cascade
range to the Blue Mountains on the East, which
last may be roughly said to form another North and
South dividing-line through the State.

The climate differs materially from that of the
Western division of the State; it is far drier through
the year, and considerably colder in winter. Snow
often lies, for from three to six weeks in the months
of December and January, several inches deep, on

the level plateaus and in the valleys; while in the passes of the Cascade mountains it is often twelve and fifteen feet deep. The mails are carried through the passes in the winter time by horsemen, carriage and waggon traffic being then impracticable, and occasionally the drifts are too deep for horses to get through, and runners on snow shoes are then employed.

But it must not be supposed that even in Mid or in Eastern Oregon the climate is severe or disagreeable when tried by our English standards. The spring begins in February and lasts till May; while the weather is warm and pleasant, and the vegetation starts everywhere into life under the influence of the abundant rain. And the summer, though hot, is not sultry or oppressive, for the air is clear and crisp.

The summer and autumn are both dry, and rain seldom falls until the end of October. During the late summer and autumn the mountains are the resort of numbers of the farmers of the Willamette valley and their families, as well as of the store-keepers from the cities and towns. Packing their stores into one of the long narrow waggons of the country, and not forgetting the rifle, shot-gun, and " fish-pole " (Oh ! that Farlow or Chevalier could see the implement !) the whole family shut up house in the valley and start for the mountains. Very likely they may be four or five days on the road; as the pair of horses, willing though they be, cannot average more than from fifteen to twenty miles a day. At night they pitch a thin tent for the females, and the men and boys sleep, rolled in their blankets, round a huge camp-fire.

Arrived in the mountains, they choose some favourite dell, high up, with a cool spring babbling over the rocks at one side, and a clear sward, on which the two horses are picketed, in front. The waggon is unpacked, the tent pitched, the stores arranged, and the family disperse; the men to hunt the black-tailed deer, and later on in the season the elk (wapiti) and the black bear. The boys find a lake near by filled with trout, large and small, and perseveringly fish with a clothes' prop, a cord, and a bunch of worms, and catch, not much. The women and children fill huge baskets with the mountain berries, which they boil down into jam for winter use, the black pot being always kept simmering on the cross sticks over the fire.

And so they pass three, four, or five weeks, in the clear sunny mountain air, till the harvest in the valley is ripe.

That this holiday is generally enjoyed may be judged from the fact that one hundred and fifty waggons of campers-out paid toll, as we were told, in one season, at one gate in a pass on the Willamette and Cascade mountains military-waggon road.*

The soil of Mid Oregon varies extremely. On the summit of the table-land, east of the Cascades, are wide tracts covered with fine volcanic ash. Wherever this is watered by one of the many streams issuing from the mountain sides, and fed from glaciers or winter snows, heavy crops of natural grass, and if cultivated, of grain, are raised.

Horned stock do exceedingly well on these wide plains, which are not bare, but are broken in many places, with groves and belts of splendid firs, pines, and cedars.

The herdsmen buy in the valley from the farmers large numbers of calves, giving from 1*l.* to 1*l.* 10*s.* for each. Collecting them into bands of from 200 to 500 or more in number, they drive them in short journeys over the mountains and there leave them to nature, taking their chance of a winter of only ordinary severity. In average years the cattle thrive even through the winter months, and require no artificial feeding ; and in twelve months each calf has doubled in value, and in two years will be ready to sell to go east at from 4l. to 6l. The herdsman has to rough it, leading on horseback a solitary life, or having but one or two companions as wild as himself, guarding his band of cattle as nights grow cold, and berries scarce, from a roving bear—and keeping off the coyotes, the small wolves which hunt in packs, and the more dangerous large grey wolves which either alone or in twos and threes grow bold from hunger. But these men will tell you that they enjoy the freedom of this unfettered life ; and the sight of their vigorous figures, rough red and brown faces, easy motions, and independent style, makes the visitor from the East come near to envying them.

Farther east from the mountains lie wide stretches of alkali plains, covered with low growths of sage brush (Artemisia). No elements of fertility are want-ing if only irrigation can be provided. In the Ochico valley this has been done, and excellent crops result. No doubt as population increases, far more of this

land will be brought under the plough, and then the
roads and water carriage will be improved.   At present there is little temptation for the farmer in this
district to raise more grain than his own family and
passing travellers can consume, on account of the
distance from markets and the ruggedness of the
roads.

Following eastward the course of the Malheur river,
by the military-waggon road above referred to, Eastern
Oregon proper is reached.*

A succession of fine valleys is traversed — Long
Hollow Valley, Beaver Creek Valley, Buck Creek
Valley, Silver Creek Valley, Harney Lake Valley, are
passed in turn.

This last is some sixty miles wide, by more than
one hundred miles long.   One who has often travelled
this road told us that you ride for many miles where
the wild grains are higher than your head on horseback.   He describes this valley as a perfect land of
promise for farmers in the not distant future—rich
deep soil, abundant water, splendid timber on the
slopes framing in the bottom lands, and mountain
ranges in the distance to give variety to the view.

There is a station of the United States Army at

Camp Harney. The soldiers have sown some splendid fields of oats and barley, while vegetables of the finest kinds flourish in the gardens, cabbages of twenty pounds weight being not uncommon.

The forests and woodland in Oregon cover about one-fourth of the total area of the State, according to the Report of the United States Commissioner for Agriculture for 1875. The Cascade mountains, the Coast range, and the Callapoia mountains, as well as many of the smaller ranges in Western Oregon, produce thick growths of fir, pine, spruce, cedar, hemlock, larch, and laurel, while the woods in the valleys contain oak, ash, maple, balm, and alder.

The same commissioner tells us that "in the Northern part of the State the red fir abounds, and often measures 200 to 250 feet in height, with trunks nine feet in diameter, clear of branches up to 100 to 150 feet. Out of such trees 18 rail cuts have been made, and 5,000 to 10,000 feet of lumber. Alder stalks from 18 to 30 inches in circumference, hazel bushes from 1 to 5 inches in diameter are of common occurrence. Lumber is cut from alder saw logs, measuring 20 to 30 inches in diameter. In the forests south of the Umpqua the yellow pine is found, as also an abundance of sugar pine, the wood of which is in great demand. For commercial and industrial purposes, the red cedar, red fir, hemlock, and sugar pine, maple, and ash, are the most valuable."

Veneers made from Oregon maple were exhibited at the Centennial Exhibition of 1876. They were universally admired, and awarded a medal and diploma "for" in the words of the judges approved by the commissioners, " rare beauty, extreme fineness of grain, beautiful polish, toughness of fibre, and of great value for ornamental and cabinet work."

The streams running through the valleys where these grand trees grow have already been set to work in too many places to drive saw-mills. The planks and logs produced find a ready sale, not only in the State, but also in California. Rough, red, and yellow fir lumber fetches at San Francisco twelve dollars per 1,000 cubic feet; spruce and white fir eighteen dollars; white cedar, oak, maple, and ash, fifty dollars. The lumber-men buy the wood as it stands, paying for each tree so much for "stumpage," varying from fifty cents to one dollar a tree.

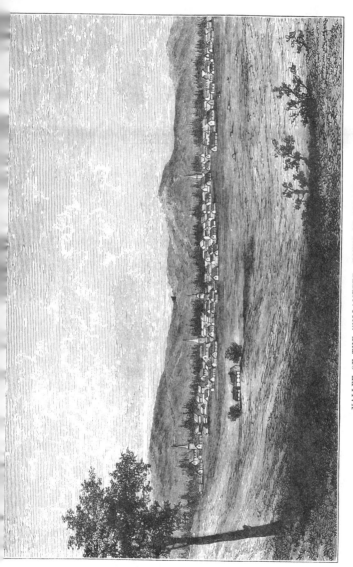

VALLEY OF THE WILLAMETTE—TOWN OF ALBANY.

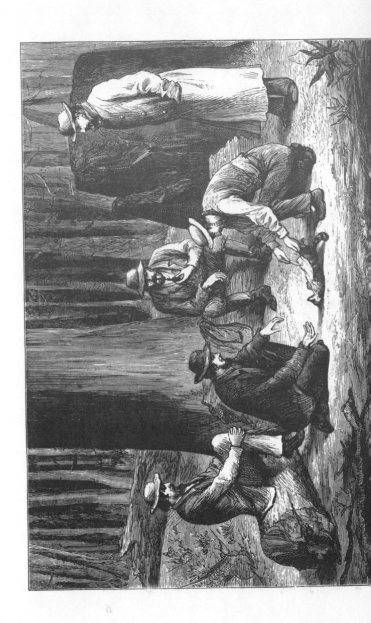

CHAPTER VI.

THE previous chapter of general description will properly introduce the history of our own travels on foot, horseback, in waggon and train, through the Western part of Oregon.

We fitted out our expedition at Corvallis, and there engaged probably the best horsekeeper and the worst cook in the State.   Horses were hired from the "Livery and Feed Stable" in the main street, and half the loafers and idlers in the town clustered round us to watch the selection of six horses out of about twenty standing there, presenting a series of groggy hind-legs and rough coats and tails down to their heels for us to choose from.

Each traveller suited himself. The Colonel picked out a narrow, high-bred iron-grey, which had been brought into the town a fortnight before by a rogue of a horse-jockey to win a "running" race. The

K

mare had been beaten, and her owner sold her to
the livery-stable keeper for forty dollars. Not a
high price, 8*l.*, to give for a thoroughbred four-
year-old, sound in wind and limb! But she shied,
and was the innocent cause of a great list of strange
oaths, and curses not loud, but deep, for the next
few weeks, as a sudden jump half across the narrow
road shook the Colonel well up in his seat from
time to time, and ended generally with a smart
stroke across the ears for the mare, and a wild
tear for a few hundred yards, sending the dust flying
in clouds over the unhappy comrades quietly pacing
behind.

The Captain's horse was a quiet and well-behaved
bay, who took a serious view of life as a rule, but
did not mind a canter for a mile or so if the road
were but level.

The naturalist's horse was a deceitful beast. He
looked as sedate and sober-sided as his rider; but
there was a reserve of devilment which broke out
twice: once as horse and man were passing a
campers' waggon in a narrow, climbing road, with
a sharp fall of fifty or sixty feet to the river below,
when a wild bout of kicking and scrambling on the

edge ended, luckily, in the horse's regaining his footing on the road; and a second time in a still worse fit, on a still more precipitous edge, when the fight was finished by the horse getting rid of his rider in the dusty road, and galloping madly back, to be caught by the Colonel and the lawyer five or six miles behind.

The lawyer had last choice, but the beast turned out well; he walked fast, and was sure-footed as a mule on the mountain-tracks; but such a wriggle he gave whenever he was urged to trot or canter! Truly there was a "screw loose" in his hind quarters, which never went in time with the two fore-legs.

The men and horses being hired, the next thing was to get guides and waggons.

One word, though, for the cook. He was a student at the college, and volunteered for the trip. He said he could cook very well. But his taste was not our taste; and after two days we all rebelled against hard chunks of beef, fried; potatoes, fried; coffee all grounds; and bread all dough and burn; but still he said he could cook very well, and objected to cook and wash-up dishes and plates for the horsekeeper and the guide.

We had a great debate: stove or no stove? Ultimately a portable iron stove was made for us in Corvallis in one day, and it was carried all through the trip.

Fancy the face of the ironmonger in any little quiet English market-town on being told he must plan out, put together, and turn out complete, an iron stove, of a different pattern from any in his shop, with fire-place, oven, boiler, chimney, damper, hot-plate, and all in a space of three feet by two, in twenty-four hours! He would promise it to you for next week, and then apologise for not having finished it, and keep it a fortnight longer in hand. Our American ironmonger took the order about eleven o'clock in the day, suggested several sensible alterations, promised the stove by eight o'clock the next morning, and delivered it at our door by seven.

Then we bought self-rising flour, potatoes, bacon, and other necessaries, and thick grey blankets, Oregon make, for each, and our outfit was ready. But we had a day to spare in Corvallis, and so we three Englishmen took our "fishpoles" out to try for the trout in the Mary river.

We hired a pair-horse buggy and were driven out

west some six miles till we came to Philomath, a
little scattered village just at the edge of the coast
range, where the hills sink into the level of the
Willamette valley.

We passed many fields of wheat and oats, just
ripening for harvest, with the red soil showing where
the road was cut into the hill-side, and copses and
woods of oak, ash, maple, cherry, and hazel; then,
noticing two fields of hops (one of which looked up
to the Kentish standard), we reached the village. A
large, red-brick school-house,[*] where forty pupils of
the better class are lodged and taught, stood on a
little slope north of the village, and close by ran the
line of the Corvallis and Yaquina Bay railroad, where
several ploughs and a fair number of men were at
work "grading."

Our road passed on among the hills, very like that
from Moreton Hampstead to Chagford, in our Devon,
but with the mass of Mary's Peak, 4,000 feet high,
in place of the 1,700 of the Dartmoor Cawsand.
Presently we came to and crossed the first bridge on
Mary's river, near which stood a white flour mill.
The stream ran boldly over a rocky bottom, with
ripples and pools alternating, and overhung with

copse on one side, the meadows belonging to two
little farm-houses fronting the river on the other side.

The houses stood on a thick trunk some two feet
high at each corner, the house looking complete in
itself, and just laid on its four supports.

Our driver drew our attention to this style of
building, and observed, "That is a handy way of
building for a fellow that is not very particular."
"Why?" "Well, I'll tell you. I knew a man that
borrowed five hundred dollars on his place, and the
man gave him notice to pay off. So what does he
do but, next Sunday, when the folks were all at
church, he gets a lot of fellows with ropes and
tackle, and he puts his house on to rollers, and
off they run with it; and the next morning, when
his friend came after his money, never a house was
there!"

The river here turned abruptly to the North, and
and ran out of sight round a high, timber-covered
bluff, while the road followed the valley westwards
for about four miles, till it struck the river again
at another bridge. The country here was rugged
and broken, a heavy belt of timber and bushes
fringing the river, and the hills drawing closer and

rising more abruptly, covered with thick yellow grass and with little scattered oak and fir copses in places.

We left the buggy to go back to the first bridge and wait for us there at seven o'clock, it being now just noon. The sun was hot, the sky cloudless, and scarcely any breeze stirring; so we three strangers put our rods together and sat down under a tree to eat our lunch, prudently keeping a crust for tea-time.

Then we parted, to meet at the lower bridge. The stream was so wooded that wading was the only way to reach the water. The captain put on a minnow boldly at once and forced his way straight down stream, choosing the holes and deeps, and leaving his companions to the temper-trying labour of fly-fishing in a wooded stream, with a good deal of still water and no breeze.

The lawyer put on a "black palmer" and a "blue upright," and set off to see if these old favourites would not tempt an Oregon trout as well as an English, Scotch, or Norwegian.

A sandy bank ran out into the stream, and the water rippled over its edge, forming a nice dark

pool on the lower side; so, softly stepping into the
water, and getting the flies well into play under
the thick trees which came down only too near the
water, they fell gently on the edge of the ripple
and curled round on to the run below. Swish! at
the very first cast, up came a trout at the tail-
fly; but, alas! he came short, and the bough was
only three feet or so from the water!

Patience and a few gentle tugs set the line free,
with no damage done. The pool held another trout,
though, which could not resist the sight of the
foreign flies; he turned out a nice plump fellow of
about a quarter of a pound, and lived under the
roots of the old tree at the lower end. The water
was quite warm; and it was like old times to feel it
flowing quickly against one's ankles in the shallows,
and more gently in the quiet reaches, while the
trees met almost always overhead. The great king-
fisher flitted across the pools and perched on a dead
bough, quite tamely, near us; and we came suddenly
on a wild duck with brown plumage and black bill,
and a whole brood of little fluffy ducklings, terribly
upset by so unlooked-for an intrusion.

The channel got more rocky as we passed slowly

down, picking up a trout here and there out of the
eddies and under the great stones. The banks became
higher, till from the stream we could see the tall firs
above, looking over the heads of the alders, hazels,
and maples, forming the brushwood by the river.

Our companions had been lost sight of hours ago,
and the shadows on the water lengthened, while
the sun's heat grew less, the water darkened in
colour, and the wooded banks seemed to press closer.

The river now led us into a gorge, where the pools
were deep, and we had to jump from rock to rock,
and force the way under one or two dead firs, which
had fallen from above and lay across the stream.

The river turned and twisted round the steep hill-
sides till it seemed impossible to say which direction
it was taking. The rod was taken to pieces, and all
the fisherman's thought given to getting out of the
place where every minute it was harder to get along.
Pushing a way through the dense wood we emerged
into a little meadow with high hills circling it round,
only to find a great short-horned bull, at the head of
eight or nine cows equally well-bred, fronting us, and
pawing the ground. Getting back to the water just
in time to get out of the way of a charge of the

whole band which came blundering through the scrub, we tried again the river-road for a time.

The light was going fast, the gorge got deeper and wilder, and a night in the woods was in prospect. There was light at any rate for some time on the hill-sides, so we took to the high ground, and mounted to the top only to find other hill-tops all round, and not a trace of house, fence, road, or track.

The compass showed the direction of Corvallis, and we set out to get as far as possible before night actually fell, meaning then to build a fire, broil some trout, and camp for the night.

It got darker and darker, until the distant land-marks disappeared, and we stumbled along as best we could. Just as we were choosing the tree for a fire we struck in the dark on a wheel-track in the grass—followed it for a mile or so to a woodstack, where a huge tree had been cut down and split up— then found a log fence, and felt our way along it down the hill-side. After what seemed an interminable time, a white house loomed up in the dark night, and while we were wondering how soon the pack of dogs about the farm would open on us, a cheery voice cried, "Is that you?" and we found our party united again at the bridge at half-past nine instead of seven o'clock.

We got back to Corvallis to a very welcome supper at half-past eleven, and could then afford to laugh at our first experience of trout-fishing in Oregon. By the by, we found that we had each taken fifteen or sixteen fish, and that the bag was larger than the natives expected for themselves when they went out a-fishing.

The next day the expedition started.[*] We had our first experience of the Mexican saddle, with high pommel and back, and enormous stirrups, and here we confess that if the English saddle is pleasant for a short ride, we should very strongly prefer the Mexican for a journey.

We came for camp into a patch of green by a grove of large trees, not far from Philomath, the starting-place for our yesterday's exploits. The horses were picketed, each with a sheaf of half-ripe oats, cut from the nearest farmer's field (and *well* charged for) and the much talked-of stove was set to work. But if the stove gave us more things to eat, yet we all sighed for the great camp fire, which after this first night was always blazing.

After supper each man chose what he thought would be the softest spot, and there laid his roll of blankets down. Mr. Abbey (commonly, but not disrespectfully, called "Kit Abbey," after his former mate and leader, Kit Carson, with whom he had lived and fought for many a year "on the plains") picked out a little hollow under a bush for his lair. He said he liked these sheltered places, as the leaves kept off the dew. The rest got their beds ready in the open, just away from the overhanging trees.

The naturalist turned out with the shot gun, a heavy 12-bore, one barrel loaded with bird-shot, the other with buck-shot. Kit Abbey's two hounds spied the gun and slunk off too, and they disappeared through the bushes and crossed the river. Presently we heard a distant shot, and both hounds gave tongue. Kit Abbey jumped up from the ground, pipe in mouth, seized his rifle, and ran off; while the deep voice of the young hound and the lighter notes of the old spotted dog echoed all round the hills in the still evening air. The hunter posted one of us, rifle in hand, at one ford, to watch, and was out of sight in a moment, towards the next pass higher up.

We stood watching there some time, listening to

the hounds' voices growing fainter in the distance, but we were only disturbed by a heron which had been fishing in the stream just out of sight, suddenly splashing in the water and flapping through the branches.

Just before we lay down a neighbouring farmer came in for a chat. Amongst other details, he told us that he had employed a number of Chinese in clearing his ground of oak scrub, the stems of which were as thick as a man's thigh. The cost was from seven to nine dollars (1*l.* 8*s.* to 1*l.* 16*s.*) an acre, but the first year's crop paid for the clearing, and left a good profit besides.

Being all well tired, each wrapped his blankets round him, and went to bed on the grass; the horses picketed round. The air was cool and sweet, the stars bright overhead. We slept soundly, our saddles for pillows, the sound of the horses grinding up their oats for our lullaby.

In the morning the mist lay round us, the night dews having been so heavy that our hair and our blankets were soaking wet, yet no one took any harm, and this was our experience throughout.

The bath in the nearest pool in the river the next morning was a delight to recall. It is true that our

American friends looked on in half-wonder, half-ridicule, with no desire to emulate.

We looked in vain for the two hounds; they had followed their deer across the ridge some miles off, and had "watered" him in the stream which ran down that valley, and we did not recover them for two or three weeks afterwards; much to our regret and to the infinite disgust of Kit Abbey. He had promised himself the pleasure of seeing us kill both deer and elk on the trip, as the deer abounded near every halting place, and the elk were to be found about this time in the higher ranges of the hills we were to cross on our way to the ocean.

The next day we passed a fine stretch of farming country only partly occupied; the lower ground fit for all kinds of corn; the upper slopes, covered with thick grass, adapted to carry both cattle and sheep.

The evening brought us to a lovely valley, called King's Valley, on the Luckiamute.* We camped close by the river, in the shade of timber, and near by a saw-mill, with the rushing of the water over the mill-dam in our ears.

The sawyers had cleared a good many of the splendid firs; there were several rafts of the trunks in the mill-head; but we looked up from the river-side into many acres of timber, most of which measured from four to six feet in diameter, six feet from the ground, and gave nearly 100 feet in the clear before the straight run of the stem was broken by a single branch. These trees were chiefly the red fir, and were worth from 1 dollar to 1 dollar 50 cents per 1,000 cubic feet, when felled, and when sawn, 10 dollars per 1,000 feet superficial, 1 inch thick.

Some of this fir-covered land is worth 300 dollars to 500 dollars an acre with its trees.

The finest timber grows on the best land, so the settler with capital chooses the thickest and strongest timber yet open to selection, fixes on a site on the stream where he can get a head of water, puts up a saw-mill and builds his log-house. In two or three years he has doubled his capital, and has his land for farming free.

The next day we camped near the new farmhouse of Mr. Meade,* a settler of twelve years history. His house stood in the heart of a large tract which had been swept by a forest fire forty years ago. For fifteen or twenty miles we passed among the huge, black standing trunks which had survived the fire, and

resisted the slow decay which had brought down many
of their neighbours, now rotting into red and yellow
soil among the thick fern and wild pea-vines. From
a hill-top, looking on a wide prospect of this fire-
ravaged land, the distant stems reminded us of a
forest of masts standing in crowded docks. It was
only by drawing close to one of these scarred trunks
that one could realise its size—five or six feet thick,
and ninety or a hundred feet high. A young growth of
alder is stretching along the river banks and mossy
hill-sides, and firs, fifteen to twenty years old, are
growing in wide strips along the hills.

One of our party drew a little in water colours,
and to Mr. Meade's great delight sketched for him
his fine new white house, standing on a slope away
from the road, with several good fields of oats and hay
round, and an attempt at a garden with gooseberry
and currant bushes, and a fair show of vegetables, in
front. He was very anxious to have all the children,
as well as the heads of the family, introduced, so a
bench was brought out and ranged along the house,
and a row of five healthy, curly-headed children, put
into the picture. This was to go to the old folks
in Illinois "to show them what sort of a place ours

is. And now, Mister, what have I got to pay? I
reckon it ain't fair to take up your time for nothing,
and I'm willing to do the thing that is right."

The fame of our artist's accomplishments spread.
The next morning, before breakfast, as we were sitting
round, a handsome young farmer rode up on a bare-
backed horse, in grey work-a-day clothes, and with
three axes on his shoulder he was going to get
ground.

A picturesque figure, as any artist could wish for,
he cantered into the middle of our party, and, suddenly
checking his horse, sung out, " Which of you fellows
it the man that takes photographs ? If he wants to
take me, I'm his man."

The sketcher made haste to get his book and colour-
box ready, and told him to sit still for a minute or
two. But that was not his idea. " Hold hard a
bit," he cried; " I guess I'll get myself fixed up a
bit before I have my picture taken." In vain the
artist told him to stay where he was, and that as he
was and no otherwise would his picture be taken.

Off he cantered, his axes clattering, his hair streaming freely under his rough hat. In about twenty
minutes back he galloped, and reined up proudly

L

among us just as we had finished breakfast. What a
change! a shiny suit of black clothes, bought ready
made and no fit; a white shirt, a bright blue silk
tie, a purple riband round his neck, with a great white
metal Centennial medal; another medal, some tem-
perance badge, pinned to his waistcoat; his hair
combed out straight and oiled. "*Now* I guess I'll
do," he cried out. No one moved; the artist went
on quietly splicing a broken fishing rod.

After sitting there on his horse for a minute or
two, he called again, "Where's the photographer?"
No one answered. He waited again, and at last the
idea struck him that people sometimes meant what
they said. So, with a parting observation, "I guess
some fellows can't judge when a man's best looking,"
he rode off.

We crossed the divide the next day, and struck
the head of the Yaquina River, running to the Pacific.
We passed the old trail made by General Phil Sheridan
in 1857, from Fort Hoskins to the Siletz Indian agency.
The path is overgrown; some beavers had thrown
their dam across the little stream that ran close by,
and had overflowed the road, and turned it into a
reedy swamp. Fort Hoskins* has been long ago

abandoned, and wheat is growing on the parade ground. There is no hostile Indian within hundreds of miles, and certainly no fear on the settlers' part of the remnants of the scattered tribes now settled on the Siletz reservation, which provide at hay time and wheat harvest much needed help to the white men farming all around.

The next day we camped at Wilcox's,* a pretty glade by the river-side. The wild gooseberry bushes, covered with small, purple fruit, grew in clumps.

We passed Mr. Trapp's* farm, a model of what an energetic, sensible farmer can get together in Oregon. About nine hundred acres of land, of which one-third was flat, bottom land by the river, and the rest running up the slopes of the hills round — good crops of oats, potatoes, fruit, and vegetables—a flock of two or three hundred sheep— a large herd of horned stock—a good house and a garden full of flowers—altogether made up posses- sions of which many hundred farmers struggling here in England to make both ends meet, and ground between the mill-stones of rent and tithe on the one hand, and grumbling, striking farm-labourers on the other, might well be envious.

The next day the ground was more broken and the hills higher; the road wound up the hillsides overlooking the river a hundred feet below, the vegetation growing always fuller and richer as we neared the ocean. Our naturalist had two escapes. We had to pass two waggons of campers returning from their holiday by the beach to their inland farms. The road was very narrow and the ground precipitous on the left. The horse got restive in passing the others, and set to kicking on the edge: we who were behind looked with dismay at his hind-legs getting nearer the edge at each plunge, until they slipped over; the stones and dust flew, and we expected the next moment to see horse and rider roll helplessly down to the river. A tremendous struggle landed them again on the road, and all was well.

Late in the afternoon, as the colonel and the lawyer were quietly jogging along the road running between woods, a horse's feet clattered towards them at a furious pace. He came into view directly afterwards, galloping with a broken bridle round his neck, and halter trailing in the dirt; no saddle, and one side covered with dust and gravel from a

recent fall. They stopped him, and recognised the
same brute which had had the kicking bout earlier
in the day.

But where was his rider, and what catastrophe
had happened? So leading and driving the runaway, they set off, and hurried along. It was some
four or five miles before they recognised in the
dusty road the print of a nailed shoe, showing a
firm and steady tread; so their anxieties were ap-
peased, and they went on more leisurely till they
overtook the naturalist trudging steadily along towards the Bay. The horse had set to kicking and
plunging furiously at the very highest and most
dangerous part, and, after a well-fought struggle,
had succeeded in depositing his rider on his back
in the road, and had dashed off along the road
backwards. Probably by rushing through the wood
he had got rid of saddle and bridle.

But thoughts and words were diverted at once
by the view which suddenly broke on us as we
reached this highest point.

Through the red stems of the lofty firs, and across
a wooded valley, over two lower ridges covered with
smaller firs and the richest undergrowth of ferns,

rhododendron, laurel, and whortleberry, we saw a land-locked, winding bay. We looked right over the low hills forming its westward bounds out to the Pacific, lying calmly, meriting its name, in the evening sun, by whose rays the whole prospect was glorified and brightened.

Each one gazed silently and long at a scene too lovely ever to forget; and quietly we found our way through the thick vegetation down towards the sea-level.

Soon two or three white houses peeped out from the hillside on the north, the road wound steadily downwards, and along an edge almost deserving the name of a cliff overhanging the water, and our party met at the little hotel at Newport, on Yaquina Bay, the farthest western point of our wanderings.

In the evening we turned out for a walk. The sea-breeze blew chilly in our faces as we climbed to the old lighthouse, and saw Cape Foulweather on our right to the north, a bold headland on which the seas were breaking, and beneath us a ridge of black rocks running straight out from the land, and sheltering the entrance to the harbour. We passed several camps of holiday-makers, their white tents

YAQUINA BAY.

YAQUINA BAY—INDIANS' FULL DRESS.

planted among the bushes on the cliffs, with little broken ravines giving access for each camp to the sandy beach below.

When we got back to the hotel night had fallen.

Here and there, across the bay, flitted lights; each shone from the torch blazing in the stern of a canoe, in which sat an Indian, spear in hand, watching for the fish.   As one came nearer to the land, the figure of the Indian came into view, and his action, as he rapidly and surely drove his light spear at the great flounders and raised them writhing and struggling on its point.

The next day we hired one of the two pilot cutters in the harbour, and sailed six or seven miles up the Channel.   Like all Pacific harbours there is a bar at the mouth, in this case about half-a-mile wide.

There seems to be about sixteen feet on the bar at low tide, with a rise of seven feet eight inches at the worst; so that the harbour, as it is, is open to the coasting craft, and to steamers of light draft of water.

But Nature has provided in the rocky ridge on the north, and in a row of rocks lying about a mile off parallel with the land, a sure and easy method of improvement.   It did not seem to us to need much expenditure of skill or money to dredge and blast from

the bar and sand-banks, enough material to deposit on
and between the rocks, and form a solid breakwater,
and thereby a safe and noble harbour for the largest
ships.

It is to be hoped that the United States Government will spend there, so much of the Pacific coast-
harbour appropriation, as will render Yaquina Bay a
safe harbour of refuge, already so much needed between
San Francisco and the Columbia.

Turning up the Bay, and towards the inflow of the
Yaquina River, we passed the oyster beds.   The old
oyster-man came off to us in his boat, and sold us for
a dollar a sack full of tender little natives, plump and
white.   Till we got back to Newport, we kept three of
our number, who were ill-advised enough to exhibit
their talent, hard at work opening oysters, and thereon
we all feasted, without brown bread and butter.

We drifted gently along with the stream down the
harbour, and a fish-hawk, after circling round two or
three times, settled on the branch of a dead tree,
showing out clear against the sky, about 150 yards
from the boat.   Some one said to Kit Abbey, "There's
a mark for you, Kit!" and handed him his rifle, which
was lying in the bottom of the boat ready for the seals,

which had several times showed their sleek black
heads.

Kit lazily took the rifle, and just dropped it into his
hand towards the bird, and fired with an instantaneous
aim.   The bird, hard hit, swung round the branch on
which it sat, and hung a moment by its claws.   He
shot again in the same quick way, and the poor bird
dropped dead on the mud.   We tried in vain to get it,
that it might be brought to England and stuffed, for
the mud was too deep to cross.

But what a dangerous foe this man would be, with
his imperturbable coolness and unerring sight.   His
life is quiet enough now, but what a book he could
write, if he would but tell of his wild time past.   He
was one of Fremont's guides across the mountains in
his reckless march, and passed many years on the
frontier, warring with " hostiles," hunting the buffalo
alone, with a few white comrades, or with friendly
Indians ; sporting, fighting, love-making, card-playing,
trapping, guiding—into one month sometimes crowding
more incident and adventure than some of us meet in
our whole lives.

When we got back to the hotel, and had dined, we
were invited to a friendly dance.   We said that we

were not well dressed enough to dance, but that we would go and look on.

Over the whole length of one of the three or four stores extended the ballroom, about fifty feet long, and five and twenty wide, it was lighted with candles, in tin sconces on the walls, and hung with wreaths of green and flowers. At the far end there was a platform, and on it the musicians were sitting—a harp, fiddle, and cornet.

But the feature, a little strange to us, was the conductor, who sat in the middle of the platform overlooking the room, and gave his orders to the dancers in a loud voice, ringing far above the musicians, though they played their hardest.—" Now, gentlemen, advance —advance, I say—take your partners by the hand." " Turn 'em round." " Now, again." " Now, back to your places." " Now, ladies' chain." " Do you hear, sir?—ladies' chain—the other hand, sir." " Now, set to your partners, ladies." " Now, back again, and all's done."

There were about thirty couples in the room, besides a row of wallflowers, young and old. Where could they all come from? The place only held about ten houses and two inns. But the camps explained all.

The ladies wore generally well starched print or muslin dresses, and some had kid gloves. The men had their go-to-meeting clothes on, which they all seemed to wish themselves well out of. There, as sometimes here, the ladies looked the picture of happiness—the men, of awkwardness.

We stood at the doorway in the balcony, looking on for some time, and were not the only spectators, for three or four Indian men or lads crowded round us, shoulder to shoulder. They were thoroughly amused, chattering in low gutteral tones, and laughing heartily, not loudly, at the occasional entanglements some of the dancers got into in spite of the word of command of the conductor.

During the summer camping-out months there is a dance once or twice a week, the invitations being general, and the cost only a small contribution to pay for the band and the candles; the conductor was too big a man, and enjoyed his office far too much, to be paid.

The next day we spent quietly about the bay; walking along its shores, examining the rocks of which the cliffs consisted, gathering specimens of the flowers and shrubs growing thickly to the very water's edge,

sketching, talking to the campers, and picking up tale
and incidents of settlers' lives.

That evening there was another excitement in a
lecture to be delivered in the ballroom by a well
known Oregonian, a pioneer of 1849.

The room was well filled, the audience attentive.
The lecturer, a very tall, bearded man, about fifty-five
dressed in a long, flowing, brown-holland coat, and light
trousers, tucked into knee-high boots, promenaded up
and down the platform, with a hand-lamp in one hand
and his manuscript in the other. He chose " Man "
for his subject, and divided his discourse into many
heads, describing " Man " as a developed, as a thinking,
as an arguing, and as a civilised, and markedly as a
cooking animal. He threw in a good many local
points, and allusions to the politics of the State,
country, and district, which were received with hearty
applause.

There seemed to be a great deal of good fellowship
and friendliness among all these people. We heard
that the Sunday services in this same room were
equally well attended, and were provided for in turn by
any camping-out minister, to whatever denomination
he might belong.

We left Yaquina Bay and its cheery temporary
opulation with regret, and now turned our horses'
eads towards the Siletz Indian reserve. Mounting
he hills bounding the bay by a different road we
eached in the evening the reserve, where we spent
day or two.

We want to say more about the Indians and their
ays than befits the close of a chapter, and will
herefore pass this part of our journey for the
resent.

The character of the country remained the same:
roken hills, flat-topped if steep-sided, all covered
ith fern and wild peas up to and over their sum-
its, occasional belts of fir timber, and gullies or
w ravines filled with a thick bush of alder, elder,
urel, wild cherry, arrow bush, syringa, thimble ber-
es, salmon berries, wild cucumbers—level bottoms
y the river and streams, with here and there a
eaver swamp; fine, sunny, unclouded weather all
ay, warm but breezy, the nights bright starlight,
ut with heavy dews; this followed us throughout.

The Californians call Oregon the "web-feet"
ountry, and say it is only good for frogs and ducks.
But all things go by comparison, and they do not

know our English climate, with its average of on
hundred and fifty rainy days in the year.

To an Englishman, the Oregon climate, at any rat
in Benton county, seemed simply the most delightfu
and healthful in the world.

After two or three days travelling along a roa
about ten miles to the north of the road by whic
we went out to Yaquina Bay, we passed a farn
where a settler named Towner stood waiting for u
as we passed.

He stopped us to ask if we had a geologist in th
party. Our naturalist responded to the call. Ou
friend told us that he had found four or five mile
off, "at the head of Depot Slew (Slough) "*an ou
crop of coal, of which he showed us specimens, an
he wished us to go with him to investigate. So w
told him to come to our camping-place on th
following day, and we would go with him.

Soon after breakfast he appeared, with a pac
swung across his shoulders and a roll of blanket
He carried a pickaxe in his hand.

We packed our blankets and food for twenty-fou
hours on Kit Abbey's old white Indian pony, an
started, the party consisting of the naturalist, th

lawyer, the United States surveyor, and Mr. Towner the settler.

This last was a type of a large class—a tall, gaunt, sober-looking man, with black hair and eyes and sallow complexion; his head, filled with a smattering of knowledge on all points, but with the strongest opinions on everything we discussed, lazy beyond belief in daily life, neglecting his farm and his family, but ready at any time for exertion in any direction but that in which his duty lay.

He said that he knew the "trail" to this coal, but he "guessed" it was something overgrown by now, since he thought no one had been up since he "blazed" it out last year.

We were to sleep at a new built cabin among the woods at a clearing in course of being made by an old man lately come.

After passing along the road to the Siletz reserve for two miles or so, between fern-covered hills, we turned off to the left into the woods, and before long were buried among the great firs. The trail got fainter and fainter and soon disappeared, the hills grew steeper and the cover thicker, and before long we found ourselves forcing our way through the bushes,

then up a hill as steep as the roof of a house, then
diving into the valley, then crossing a beaver swamp
where the water gurgled and swished round our boots
and the old pony sank in knee deep. Then up anothe
hill, and another, till Towner confessed himself fairly
lost.

At last, Mr. Mercer, the surveyor, took the com
mand of the party, and after questioning Towner
closely as to points and directions, he took a line and
stuck to it, which before long brought us to a new
settler's cabin.

The cabin was surrounded by log fences, as usual
and the path led through two of these. A gap had
been made in one ; it was necessary to take down a
length of the other to get the pony through. Towner
was leading the way, his hands in his pockets. The
naturalist had his hands full, the lawyer carried his
rifle, Mr. Mercer had Towner's pickaxe, of which he
had incautiously relieved the owner.

Seven logs, eight feet long and a foot thick, are not
light, and we lowered the top three with a little diffi
culty. Towner stepped over, and passed on three or
four steps, and then turned round to look on at his
friends pulling the other logs down for the pony to

pass. So the lawyer called out, "Come, Mr. Towner, lend us a hand." With a sly look; but without a smile, he half turned away, saying, "I guess I'll '*boss*' (over-see) that job," and left the visitors to finish it. A world of character shone out in that expression; and "I guess I'll ʰoss that job," passed with us into a proverb whenever a bit of hard work had to be done which some wished tc shirk.

After another mile or so through the forest, we heard an aᶻe ringing. Climbing another steep hill, among some of the finest firs we had yet seen in the State, we came to a clearing at the top.

A new log-cabin stood at one side. A dozen huge trees lay about, the fires yet smouldering at the roots of some of them, by which they had been brought down.

An old grey-headed man, dressed in rough clothes, but with very gentle civil manners accosted us. He knew Towner, and seemed glad to talk to some one. He told us that he had been working alone all the summer clearing a farm for his sons, who were to join him when the place was ready. He looked an insect in size by the side of the huge trees he had felled. And the man seemed utterly out ᴼf proportion with the large scale of Nature all round him.

M

The loneliness of the life he had been leading oppressed us more than it did him; for he was cheerful and bright, and when we had lighted a huge fire, he turned the conversation to religious matters, and earnestly spoke of the second advent of our Lord, which he believed to be near at hand.

He boiled our kettle and made tea for us, and after a chat we rolled our blankets round us, and lay down to sleep, under the shade of one of the great felled trunks, striving, by covering our heads and all right in, to avoid the mosquitoes which rose in swarms from the neighbouring beaver-swamp as the light faded away.

About four in the morning we said good-bye to our host, after a frugal meal of bacon and coffee, and started afresh.

We left the old pony feeding on the edge of the beaver-swamp with the old man's two cows till our return.

Our guide was now quite sure of his way; but the trail was, as he feared, overgrown, and we had hard work indeed to force our way; first, bending nearly double, we crept under the mass of tangled bushes and bines; then, when our backs were fairly broken,

we stood upright, and by main force broke through
the creepers.

We were making our way along the bank of a
little stream when we heard a large body crash
through the bushes a yard or two ahead, rush
through the water, and away up the hillside. We
knew it was a bear, and did all we could to get a
sight of him ; but although we were so near that
the mud raised by his plunge into the water was
only clearing off, we could not get even a glimpse
of him, and the pace at which he got through the
bush far outstripped ours.

By about eleven o'clock we had followed the
rivulet to its source and reached the coal. Yes,
there were two distinct seams in the bank, cropping
out with a width of about twelve inches and eighteen
inches. But it was poor stuff; and after lighting
a wood fire and getting it well under way we tried
in vain to make the coal burn. It smouldered and
got red, and turned to white ash in time, and there
was the gassy smell in the smoke which spoke of
coal, but that was all.

It appeared though that there were two or three
other outcrops in a north-west and south-east line

within a few miles; the strata are no doubt coal-
bearing, but the geologist pronounced it a tertiary
coal of poor quality, and pointed out how contorted
and broken up were the strata. He pronounced it
therefore a heavy risk to go to much expense in ex-
ploration, until, at any rate, good roads had been
made, and population had much increased.

We then turned homewards and found less difficulty
in keeping the path.

Across the stream in one place lay a huge fallen
fir. We climbed on to its trunk and paced along to
the first branches. It exceeded 120 feet in the clear;
the tree we judged to have been at least 230 feet
high; the stem was fully seven feet thick where we
climbed on it.

In these woods the air could not reach us, and
the state of boiling heat we were in was worse
than being in at cricket with W. G. Grace for one
of his fastest innings. We rejoined our party at
their camp by about five o'clock, fairly tired out.

Our horses' heads were now turned eastwards again.
We travelled back to the Willamette through a succession of smaller valleys, each with one or two white
houses dotted about it. The character of the country

was the same throughout; broken hillsides, level bottoms, flat upland plateaus, heavy, grand timber on the upper ridges; a thick undergrowth in the valleys where Nature had been left to herself, and rich vegetation everywhere.

And so at length we reached Corvallis again, without accident, and each one the stronger for the trip.*

CHITCO CHARLEY.

CHAPTER VII.

How strange is the difference of tone between the way in which the gentlemen of England who sit at home at ease speak of the Red Indians and the expressions one hears about them, without exception, from those who have made their actual acquaintance !

Most of us think of the American Indian as we have read of him in the *Last of the Mohicans* and the *Pathfinder*.

But ask a man like Kit Abbey, who has lived among them half his time, or Mr. Bagley, the Indian agent at the Siletz, whose whole life is spent in trying to influence them for good, and you hear but the same report of them.

Some little account of what we saw and heard of them on the spot may be interesting.

When we turned along the edge of the cliff towards Newport on Yaquina Bay, we saw smoke rising from several little ravines leading to the shore.

We dismounted once or twice to find out whence it came, and spied little shanties hidden away in the furze and brake. Dead bushes set in a row, a few long sticks bent round and tied together at the top, a mat or two of old, torn rugs and bits of carpet thrown over, made up the dwelling.

And one or two dusky figures with long black straight hair came out to look who was passing.

A day or two after we got Kit Abbey to go with us to pay them a visit.

Whatever language of their own they speak among themselves, most of them are familiar with Chinook, a lingo invented by the half-breeds of the Hudson's Bay Company, made up of several Indian tongues with a good many words of bastard English and some French.

This is learned by all the trappers and hunters who have much to do with the Indians. The name for an Englishman, "King George's man," indicates the time when this lingo was first adopted.

So we strolled, pipe in mouth, along the sandy

beach, and soon a strong smell of decaying fish warned us we were near an Indian camp.

Close to such a shanty as we have described a squaw was squatting on the ground. She was a woman of medium height, broad, and strongly built, dressed in an old dirty print gown, and with two or three rows of large beads round her neck; three broad bands of black paint from the corners and middle of the lips to the edge of the chin-bone, and a dab of vermilion on each cheek adorned her face. How old she was it is impossible to say.

Near her was another woman, similarly marked and dressed, with a baby about twelve months old tied into a wicker cradle, which had a band to pass across the mother's forehead when they moved house. Two small boys nearly naked, eight or ten years old, were chasing each other about the sand. A great strew of fish-heads and entrails all round poisoned the air.

The father of the family lay on the ground inside the shanty, with his head just showing in the door-way.

Six or seven flounders, each with a spear-mark in its middle, were lying on a log in the sun close by

A little fire of sticks was smouldering close by the
tent.

Dirt was everywhere ; on the persons of the Indians,
their clothes, their hut, their food. And the whole
place, with the sea-water lapping on the beach close
by, and fresh wind rustling in the leaves of the
bushes, stank worse than the meanest alley in Saint
Giles's.

They all seemed glad to see Kit Abbey, and
grinned with pleasure when he spoke to them.

It was proposed that "King George's man" should
make a picture of them.

But each one wanted to look over the artist's
shoulder, and nothing but shutting the book and
threatening to refuse the promised tobacco would
make them go back to their former attitudes. But
when once the sketch was done and they had seen
themselves on the paper and had received the tobacco,
Kaseeah, the head of the family, proposed that they
should dress up " old-fashioned Indian," and be taken
again.

So they retired into the shanty for half-an-hour or
so, and then appeared in their glory.

Kaseeah stood between his two wives, and his boy

on their right, and not one stirred till the picture was finished, proud enough of their finery.

He had stripped, to a pair of *clean* white drawers, and wore a scarlet waistband. A plume of white and magenta feathers rose high from a bead head-dress, and another plume was bound on each arm, and he carried a plume in each hand. The black bands and vermilion patches on his face were freshly touched up.

The women had black stuff petticoats, and scarlet capes round their shoulders, with rows upon rows of large blue and white necklaces hung round their necks. They also carried feathers in their hands.

The boy had drawers on and nothing else, and he had a dab of vermilion on each cheek, but no other paint, and he had a plume in each hand.

The younger woman was only sixteen years old; and Kaseeah told Kit he had only been married to her about a month. He said he had had forty wives; we asked where the rest were; he answered, "Got tired of them: turned them off."

This man was a chief of the Alcea Indians, and had been concerned in one or two outbreaks in past years; he was tame enough at last.

A few days after this we travelled up to and spent a day or two on the Siletz reserve.

The road wound among the fern-covered and fir-topped hills, and late in the afternoon we descended into a deep valley, and crossed the Siletz river, a rapid stream with rocky and gravelly bottom.

Passing between two log fences, which divided the road from the little farms of some of the Indians, we soon came in sight of the Agency—five or six wooden, one-storied houses, grouped together on a little green knoll.

When we had made our camp and lighted our fire some eight or ten of the Indians came round us. They all knew Kit Abbey, and a long and voluble Chinook conversation followed. One old man squatted a little way off quite silently, never varying posture or face. He was the oldest chief on the reserve : one of the Coquelle Indians, if we heard the name rightly. Just at sundown Kit Abbey told us to watch the old fellow, as he was going to have his sweat-bath.

He moved off quietly and we followed, past the Agency houses to a piece of green sward among the houses of the Indians. There was a round hillock, raised in the centre about two feet above the level of the ground; on one side of the hillock was a hole, framed in wood, about fourteen inches square.

The old man doffed his clothes, and squeezed himself, head first, through the hole. Soon a light appeared through another smaller hole on the other side. This light came from a heap of brushwood thrown together on a kind of shelf at one side of an underground cavity about eight feet square by six feet high in the middle.

The old Indian, having set fire to the brushwood, lay down by the side of it on the shelf, and began crooning over a most mournful ditty, he lying with his face downwards on his crossed arms.

The smoke drifted out through the smaller hole; and it was possible to live, though, we should think, hard to breathe, in the chamber. Very soon beads of perspiration shone in the firelight on the dark, copper-coloured skin, and the chant grew louder as the heat entered the old man's bones. The moisture streamed off him as the red embers glowed, and still his song went on, like no other we had ever listened to, wavering and quavering, but continuous.

We stood and watched him for ten minutes or so,

while the evening light faded away from the sky, and the white mist rose in wreaths over the grass and clover fields. Presently the old fellow rose from his shelf and struggled out of his hole and marched off, as he was, down the road for a couple of hundred yards, and then popped into a deep hole in the river and sat there for a few seconds. Then he got out, shook himself, passed his hands over his limbs, and proceeded to put on his clothes.

The surgeon in charge told us that the old man took this bath every night of his life, and that others were equally fond, though not so regular in the use, of it. The Indians prescribe it as a remedy for all complaints—very often with good results; but when an epidemic of measles visited them some few years ago they persisted in having recourse to it, and, in the doctor's words, they died like flies.

Later on in the evening we called at the house of Mr. Bagley, the Indian agent. It was comfortably furnished, and all the white inhabitants of the reserve gathered in the large sitting-room, with a bright wood fire.

The society consisted of the agent, his wife, and daughters; the surgeon, his wife, and children; the carpenter and his family; and the agent's clerk; and they were the only whites among a population nominally of 1,300, actually of 800 to 1,000 Indians.

We asked Mr. Bagley whether he had succeeded in influencing the Indians much.   He told us that he found the greatest difficulty in getting them to settle to any pursuit; that some thirty or forty of them had little farms, but only one of them had taken to cultivating the ground well.   The majority of the men employ themselves in horse-raising and selling when they are at home; many of them go about hiring themselves to this farmer or that for odd farming jobs.

They have a school, but not many go to it, and very few attend the Sunday services.

The valley in which the agency farm is situated is about six miles round, and there is an upper and a lower valley of about the same extent.

The land was exceedingly fertile, but, even when tried by an Oregon standard, the farming was ragged and careless in the extreme.

An idea has spread that the number of the Indians is rapidly decreasing now that their nomadic habits are checked, and that they are confined to the limits of the reserve. The doctor told us, however, that this was a mistake, and that the births exceed the deaths now that the purchase of spirits is impossible for them, and that their children are properly attended to in sickness.

Our friend the surgeon had lived for several years there, and his opinion was that diseases of all sorts were diminishing in intensity among them. We did not say that it was possible that his own practice might be more successful as his experience increased

Mr. Bagley described to us an outbreak among the Indians several years ago. We asked if he ever feared another. He said, No; but added that if such were to happen he knew that he would be the first victim; and the more certainly the higher the respect and affection they bore him.

Kit Abbey confirmed this afterwards, and told us that a few years ago an Indian woman named Chitco Jennie had "packed" for him and his comrades for a winter in the mountains.

When a party of hunters go into the hills for deer and bear, they prefer to have some Indian women to "pack" (*i.e.* carry) the carcases and skins down to the settlements.

Chitco Jennie had taken a leading part in the massacre of Mr. Goodchild, the Indian agent. Mr. Abbey asked her if it was true that she and her people had killed the man, cut out his heart, and had cooked and eaten it. "Yes," said she; "he was a very good man, and a brave." "Then why treat him so?" he asked. "Because," said she, "we knew that if we eat his heart we should get his courage and his goodness too."

"She is dead now," said Mr. Abbey; "but she was not a bad sort, in spite of her murderous ways. She always treated us well, and she was one of the strongest women I ever knew. I have seen that woman, sir, pack five deer on her back to the settlements: that is, carry one down, leave it, come back for another, carry that, and so on, for five; and, let me tell you, sir, a black-tail deer, even after he is cleaned, is a tough weight for a man, let alone a woman."

The next day we visited the Indian burying-ground. It was placed on the side of a hill sloping to the east, not far from the spot where the barracks of the troops stood, in the early days of the reservation.

There were many graves, each surrounded by a slender paling of upright laths, their tops roughly carved or cut into patterns. The surfaces of the graves were flat, and each had been covered with the bed-clothes last used by the deceased.

On this were arranged his or her most cherished possessions: if a man, his gun, saddle and bridle, axe, or spade: if a woman, her workbox, teapot, cups and saucers, spoons, and knives and forks. To the four corners of a child's grave were tied the tiny shoes and the little garments of the lost one.

On one woman's grave were the rusted remnants of a sewing-machine: on one chief's grave a costly rifle had been left to rust and decay.

We could not ascertain if these articles were spoiled or broken before being left, though in several instances it seemed to be the case.

The superintendent told us that often the Indian funerals were scenes of the wildest sorrow, the relatives crying and mourning loudly, and showing themselves very reluctant to leave the spot.

When the soldiers were quartered there, and before the Indians had given up all hope of breaking out and getting free again, repeated plots were laid

N

for massacre and murder. But always one or other of them warned some friend among the white men of his danger, and so the attempt was provided against.

One chief was introduced to us (the one who had taken to farming) as the Indian who had twice put the commander of the soldiers on his guard. This man, a Rogue River Indian, had fought bravely until his tribe was overpowered and beaten, and he himself taken captive; but he had admitted once for all the superior power of the white men, and had set himself to learn their arts. He had become a fair carpenter and farmer, and had naturalised himself as a citizen of the United States, being the solitary instance on the reservation.

The Indians on this reserve represented all that are now left of the following tribes:—

Rogue Rivers.	Macanotanas.
Shastas.	Multenotanas.
Klamaths.	Chitcoes.
Galeese.	Euchres.
Shasta-Costas.	Joshuas.
Coquelles.	Salmon Rivers.
Tootootenas.	Alceas.

Nestuccas.   Tillamooks.
Siuselaws.   Coos.
Umtquas.

Doubtless acts of injustice and crime have pre-
ceded the removal of these Indians from their former
possessions to their present homes : they have been
too often treated like the "coyotes," or prairie'
wolves, driven from before the settler, and killed if
they preyed on his flocks, brought only too tempt-
ingly before their eyes. But it is also fair to place
oneself in the settler's position.

Imagine him as he so often is : rough, rude,
hardy, self-confident, ambitious, and somewhat selfish.

Moved with the love of change, or desire for
broader or more fertile lands, he left the clearings
for the wilderness, family and all. He found the
promised land, and pitched his camp by some bright
stream, and there felled trees and framed his hut.

He saw no sign of occupation of the country, by
his reading of the word; no turned up soil, no flocks
and herds, no house or fence. But from a patch
of bush close by the riverside a thin blue smoke
rose, and the settler was aware of "Indian sign."

A visit showed him the native's dwelling, such as we have described it, squalid, dirty, frail; its owners, according to the white man's notions, idle, worthless, dissolute, ignorant — without the will or the power to use or develop the country they claimed.

Was he who had come from so far off to this land, and found it good, who felt that under his hands wildness would give place to cultivation, waste to usefulness, savagery to culture—was he to retire, and leave its native possessors (*tenants* rather) to themselves?

Doubtless he often thought—Let me turn this soil to use; let me make corn grow, set sheep and cattle to range these hills; let me build houses and fences, and plant schools and churches in due time here; and I will share with these Indians the benefits of the civilisation I bring; they too shall learn and prosper.

Not all pioneers set out with pistol and knife violently to disperse the native dwellers in the land, and seize their possessions for themselves, regardless of law, justice, and fair dealing.

Rather let us mark, and judge leniently, if we can, the difficulties of these scouts and outposts of civilisation, sent on by the forces of settled life in advance, to make the roads and tracks for the great army to follow. Let us remember that in the early days (and these times are but a few years back for the country of which we write) it was a life-and-death question for the early emigrant whether he and his were to be murdered, only too often foully and cruelly, or if he was to teach the Indian the danger of assailing the white man and his possessions.

One hears too much in England of the fraud and violence said to be practised against the red men by our American cousins, to possess themselves by fair means or foul of the remnants of land set apart for their habitation.

Such things may be : we saw no trace of them.

In the Siletz reserve we found, first, more and better land set apart for the Indians' use than they care to or can use; second, an " agent " in charge, who reminded us of the class of man to be chosen for the head of a reformatory, or an industrial school, or a training-ship, and therefore the most suitable for the post, so far as our judgment could go. Then from the doctor they had gratuitously medical advice and help, the results of which even now are seen in improved conditions of health : then practical

instructions in the necessary arts of house-building, farming, stock-raising; clothing and many comforts given
them; schools and teaching free, but not compulsory.

What more could the incoming white men do for
them? Save, indeed, leave them and the country to
themselves, to remain a nineteenth-century New Forest,
for the royal Indian's deer to range.

But the ten or twelve years since they were planted
on this reserve have not, we fear, yet done much good;
at any rate to the adults, whose memories are full of
the old glories of their tribes. It remains to be seen
if the race now growing up will not have so learned
their lesson as gradually to be absorbed into the society
surrounding them, where, for many years to come, every
labouring pair of hands will be so much solid gain.

The question was often put by us, Whether the
farmers disliked the presence of the Indians on their
reserve, within so many or so few miles distance from
their homestead?

The answer was invariably that the neighbours were
glad to have them as additional help at hay time and
harvest, in hop-picking, or fruit-preparing, and that
each year the number offering themselves for such
services increased.

In early years irregular alliances between the hunters of the Hudson's Bay Company and the first back-woodsmen, with Indian women, were not uncommon. We saw several half-breeds, preserving the Indian points of straight black hair, large dark eyes, and dark complexion, with the straighter foreheads and noses, and lower cheekbones and taller figures of the white man.   One very pretty half-bred woman was well married to a settler on Yaquina Bay; they had sturdy children, a good house and land; she and her children looked exceptionally clean and neat, and the house was well-ordered and comfortable.

We were told in reply to questions put to many people, in diverse conditions and places, that the Indians had many points of character in common.

All agreed that none of them were to be trusted either in the serious matter of life, or in the lesser of property.   Kit Abbey told us many tales, where in one moment the gratitude that should have been won by years of kindness had disappeared, and the Indian had killed the man who had long fed and cared for him.

The chief on the reserve, who had given warnings of the plots of his people, was the solitary exception we heard of to this general condemnation.

They are said to be very untruthful, careless, lazy, and improvident.

Their best friends speak utterly despondingly of any real change being effected in the present generation; but they are very hopeful of the rising race.

The selling or giving, or allowing alcoholic drinks to the Indians, has long been a penal offence in Oregon— a measure prompted by regard for self on the part of the colonists, as well as by care for the Indians.

KASEEAH.

CHAPTER VIII.

In the course of our travels through Oregon, we learned the history of many of the men we met.

The opportunities which the country gives may be learned from the results in individual cases, bearing in mind that the pioneers, as the earliest settlers are called, entered the State in or after 1849, and the majority of these men have achieved their present position in from fifteen to eight years back from the present time.

We will begin with a gentleman who, to use his own words, bought a farm less than seven years ago, because he found it impossible to live and bring up and educate a rising family on a salary of 1,000 dollars (200*l.*) a year as a Presbyterian minister. His estate consists of five hundred acres of land, lying on the slope of the coast range towards the Willamette valley,

and varies in character, being partly hill land and
partly bottom land.

Six years ago, when he entered on farming, he was
120 dollars in debt after he had bought his land. It has
long since been entirely free. He was utterly ignorant
of the business when he began, and was for three years
content to imitate his neighbours, ploughing, and sowing
and harvesting when they did. He learned by degrees
to walk alone, and said that he had now ventured to
bring into cultivation much land that his predecessor
considered worthless for wheat, but was this year
producing from fifteen to twenty bushels to the acre.
Much of his wheat-land yielded from forty to fifty
bushels, but his general average was brought down to
about twenty-five bushels by the new wheat-land and
by some marshy land he had not yet found time to drain.

He plants wheat at intervals from October to April,
thus insuring a gradual ripening, and rendering it
possible for him to work his farm with the help of
his two growing lads, and of the occasional aid of two
hired helps.

The profit on his wheat this year would be just
1,360 dollars, reckoning the selling-price at 62½ cents
per bushel.

He has a very comfortable eight-roomed house, a splendid orchard of twelve acres, full of fruit-trees in free bearing; finds all European fruits grow to perfection in Oregon, save peaches. But after setting apart ample supplies of fruit for household use, and making cider for the year, he was giving splendid apples to the pigs for want of a market, and was thinking of cutting down his fruit-trees and ploughing up his orchard for wheat.

This gentleman, of English parentage and education, told us that he enjoyed his life to the full. He thought he preached his frequent sermons none the worse that they were studied while he moved about his farm, drove the reaper, and shepherded his flock. We were told that the churches near were filled when he was preaching. His life is healthy, as well as happy, judging from his vigorous figure, clear complexion, and bright eye. He enjoys the respect and esteem of all his neighbours, and his services in public offices and functions are frequently sought.

One of our earliest acquaintances was a Scotch miller, who had an experience in Oregon of over twenty years. He described to us the growth and development of the State which he had witnessed,

and in which his own fortunes had shared. From
very small beginnings and early struggles, his little
wooden mill had given place to a large three or four-
storied brick building, combining a corn mill and
elevator (as the grain warehouses are called).

It was full of work when we saw it, and was driven
by the stream brought thirteen or fourteen miles from
the mountains in a canal or leat, for the use of which
he paid a heavy purchase-money. The mill stood on
the navigable river, which brought and then carried
away the corn and produce.*

We were glad to make friends with an Italian
settler, on the borders of Yaquina Bay. As we sailed
up the bay in the cutter, he came out to meet us
in his canoe from the mouth of a little stream, with
a bright-eyed, four-year-old son in the bow of his
boat.

On the slope above stood a clean white frame-house,
with quite a large clearing in front, between the house
and the bay. The fallen trunks of the great firs were
smoking here and there, the fires that were burning
them up requiring frequent tending. A vigorous young
orchard of peach, apple, and plum-trees showed two
or three years' growth at one side, and a garden full

of vegetables on the other side of the house testified
to the industry of the one pair of hands which kept
all in order.

There was a row of between thirty and forty wooden
beehives under a long boarded cover, at right angles
with the house, their inhabitants filling the air with
a familiar humming.

The owner welcomed us ashore, and with great
pride ushered us into his parlour, built, ceiled, walled,
and floored with broad cedar planks and boards, showing a grain and surface an English cabinetmaker
would have admired.

The furniture was likewise home-made.   No one
but a sailor could have been master of so many trades,
and this proved to have been our friend's original call-
ing.   He had come out about eight years before from
Italy ; had spent a year or two at the salmon fishery
in the Columbia, among many of his compatriots.
He had then fancied a season's work at farming,
had fallen in love with and married a pretty and well-
educated, half-bred girl, and had chosen a location
and settled down.

He told us that he too was contented and happy ;
that he could sell at a good price all the vegetables

and all the honey he could raise; and that fruit of all kinds, even peaches, grew and ripened well. His honey brought him, in the comb, about 2s. a pound. His stock of bees were the produce of two hives about five years ago. He had schemed out and made his "bar frame" hives, he told us, from his own ideas; certainly we saw none like them in Oregon. He moved fearlessly about among his bees, lifting out a frame here and one there, to show us the state of working.

The wife busied herself with her dishes and plates while we were in the house, keeping shyly in the background; but the rogues of children came creeping round our knees, showing the strain of Indian blood in their straight black hair and bright black eyes; but their complexions were rosy and clear, and no darker than the average of Italian children.

A few hundred yards off, on a hillock overhanging the bay, stood the original log-cabin, now degraded into a pig-sty and tool-house. Our friend had selected a quarter section of 160 acres, and had several seasons' work yet before him to bring it all into cultivation. It would be hard to find a prettier or more fertile spot.

We had some business with a lawyer in one of the little towns. We ·found him in his office, a small one-storied wooden structure, into which the door opened directly from the street. The planks of the sidewalk were rather loose in front, as was generally the case in the towns, and one tilted up occasionally and gave the sensation of walking along an ill-made scaffolding. But the fast-growing maple-trees, along each side of the road, shaded the little building; and as we sat discussing the rights of foreigners who own land in Oregon, the only disturbing sound was the rustle of the breeze among the leaves.

Our friend's library was none the less complete, that his office furniture consisted chiefly of two very old rocking-chairs and an ink-stained deal-table; while the iron stove standing out into the middle of the room held ashes of a wood fire three months old; and on talking to him we found him as well provided with law inside his head, as with orthodox-looking, calf-backed volumes on his shelves.

The heat of the day was a good excuse for his sitting in his shirt-sleeves; perhaps one felt the more lenient also to the well-smoked pipe, with blackened bowl and long stem, lying beside the old desk.

He had come westwards from Michigan twenty-five
years before, and had built up for himself, by honesty
and industry, a position of respect and confidence.
His practice was of a very miscellaneous kind; now
searching the record-books in the neighbouring court-
house and land registry, to advise on the title to
some lands ten miles off among the hills, as between
the squatter and a purchaser from an original grantee
from government; then assisting a husband to rid
himself of an "incompatible" wife in a divorce suit
easily begun, and promptly completed; then defending
in open court a lumberer charged with felling timber
on the State land without authority. Next he was
occupied in keeping the accounts and collecting the
debts of the estate of a deceased client whose will
he had first drawn up; meanwhile doing a good deal
of money-lending on a small scale, and at rates of
ten, twelve, and even more per cent. on the farms
of newcomers, or of the numerous class who were
ever adding field to field, certain that even if they
paid such rates on their mortgages, the richness of
the half-tilled soil would enable them to clear all
debt off in four or five years at most.

We went to call at our lawyer friend's house the

next morning, and found a comfortable white-painted
wooden villa, standing in a small plot of garden
ground, in a "lot" on the outskirts of the town.

A bright, pretty girl of sixteen was practising the
old "Lancers" on a very fair toned, square piano, of
Weber's manufacture, and disappeared on seeing
strangers to fetch her mother, a pleasant-faced matron,
to entertain us. She apologised for keeping us
waiting by saying she had to finish hanging out
to dry the fine things from the wash, but sat down
and chatted most pleasantly for half an hour on all
topics, from Shakespeare to the musical-glasses, showing, we thought, an amount of knowledge and reading
we should have been a little surprised at in a
similar position of life in an English county town.

And this was in a new "city" of two thousand
inhabitants, on the outskirts of civilisation, with
Indian tents on a field a mile off, and bears, wolves,
and cougars to be found by looking for them in the
mountains within ten miles.

One of the pleasantest noonday halts we made was
at the house of a very thriving farmer at a place
called Elk City, on the head waters of Yaquina
Bay.

O

The tide water ebbed and flowed through the creek
a hundred yards from the house, across the open
green. As the tide flowed, the salmon trout came
up in numbers, and our host and a friend had taken
fifteen fish, of over a pound weight each, in an hour,
very shortly before we arrived. About a dozen or
twenty little frame-houses were grouped round the
green. In front of the largest stood a maple-tree,
with round, compact head, throwing a dense shade
over the group of chairs under its branches, where
the mother of the family, a pretty grown-up daughter,
and a toddling child of three had planted themselves
to avoid the hot sun.

As our cavalcade of seven horses came into view,
our host left the boat and his fishing and came to
welcome us, and the good wife seemed to assume at
once that dinner was to be provided for all of us.
While the fowls were being roasted we sat under the
"shade tree" and cooled ourselves, and chatted.

Our friend had come to Oregon from one of the
Western States (for so in Oregon they still call Ohio
and Indiana, and Missouri, though in Oregon of
course those States lie so far to the East), about ten
years ago. He said that he and his friends made up

ELK CITY.

a settlement at first of six families, and that when they arrived in late autumn, the open valley where we sat was one mass of thick scrub, into which they had to cut their way with the axe, and not a blade of grass was to be seen. Out of their eight cows four died that first winter, and our friend looked very serious as he recalled their early struggles, and told how when that first spring came they had all but made up their minds to turn tail and give up all idea of continuing their efforts to make a settlement there. However, they "concluded to go through with it."

When we saw the place, the valley and a good way up the hill-sides had been cleared of both timber and scrub, and bright fields of oats and artificial grasses alternated with potatoes, where the haulm was nearly waist high, and not one speck of disease, not one tinge of yellow, was to be seen.

The wooden house was comfortably furnished; there were several bookshelves well filled ; newspapers lay on the table in the window ; a Yankee clock ticked loudly in the corner; and through the wide-open windows and doors the sight and scent of roses, woodbine, and sunflowers entered. Over the wide-opened yellow flowers several humming-birds were hovering, their wings and breasts flashing in the sun as they darted from place to place.

Our friend owned now over one hundred head of cattle, a large band of sheep, killed fifteen or twenty fat hogs every year, and grew from four to five tons of hay on each acre of his cleared land set apart for timothy-grass. The children were clean and well-behaved, and the general impression left was one of thrift, energy, respectability, and success.

But it is easy to find the reverse of this last sketch —and not many miles off—and our collection would not be complete without it.

After passing for several miles along a valley where clearing had hardly begun, and the tall bushes over-hung on each side, we reached a more open spot. A ragged fence of logs, some standing, some lying about, lined the road. This tumble-down fence stretched away up the hill-side. Part of the brushwood near by had been stubbed up after burning, and timothy-grass had been sowed, but the grass was mixed with weeds, and here and there lay a blackened fir-trunk, burned down but not destroyed. The efforts at clearing had failed gradually; near the road was the timothy-grass; a little way up the slope the scrub had been

cut and burned, and the weeds let grow: still a little
farther the scrub had been cut and left, and the
withered stems and branches, still upright, rested
against their growing neighbours; whilst yet above
the cut piece there was a thick belt of brush, from
which rose high in air the black trunks of the original
pines, killed by fire many years ago.

A turn in the road brought us in sight of the house,
a grey, weather-worn, one-storied cabin, looking as if
neglect and slovenliness, not age, were bringing it to
decay.

As we approached it, about three o'clock in the
afternoon, the door opened, and a man looked out.
He was tall and sallow, and had a reddish beard, sandy
hair, and small, watery, pale blue eyes. A long-
stemmed pipe hung from his mouth, and the dark
brown of the well-smoked meerschaum was the only
bit of pleasant colour about him. His clothes, down
to his boots, were of one uniform grey, and he looked
as if he had always been too lazy to wash.

We chose a grassy corner close by, where a tiny
stream showed itself by the green verge, and unsaddled.
The camp-fire was lit, the horses picketed — the
blankets got from the waggon, the potatoes washed

and set on to boil, and the bacon began to hiss in the pan, and still our friend loafed with his elbows on the fence close to the door, and smoked on.

The amateur cooks in our party prepared a stew of a couple of fowls we had bought at the last farm we passed, and in an hour or so we sat round for our meal.

Still the loafer never joined us, though two or three times we had tried to make friends. There was a good portion of our savoury food left in the pan, and one of us carried it across to the house, with a piece of fresh-baked bread and a lump of sweet, clean butter, made at the other farm that morning. But no: he guessed he didn't care for chicken, and he didn't eat butter.

His bedplace stood at one side of the room, and the dirty, touzled blankets seemed to have been but just left. A bit of rusty bacon and a hacked loaf of bread were on the shelf, and a tell-tale black-bottle near by. In the course of the evening, by dint of much tobacco and a good many dips into the whisky pannikin we got him to talk.

He had settled down there about six years ago, and had built his cabin at first. Then he had worked

hard the next two years, and had cleared the patch
of oats and timothy-grass he pointed to with his
pipe-stem.   Then, as he said, he found he had
enough to live on, with the help of a pig or two, and
a small band of cattle on the hill.   He sold his oats
and hay to passers-by, and bought flour and bacon
and whisky and tobacco.   He did not work now, why
should he ?   He was very comfortable, and he slept
a lot.   If he got tired of bacon, he could go and
shoot a deer 'most any day : but he didn't often go
after them, why should he ?   No; he didn't think he
should clear any more land; he had got enough.   If
he felt lonely he could go to the next farm, and that
wasn't above two miles off.   But he didn't often go ;
why should he ?   Yes, he went off to the town a
time or two, and had a good time, you bet ; but it
was maybe three or four months since he had gone
there, and he didn't know as he should go again.
Last year he had four tons of timothy on that patch ;
but this year only two tons and a half.   He didn't
know why it fell off.   If it went on getting worse,
he should up stakes and be off—he'd got no wife
nor child, thank God.

   We slept that night in the hay-shed as it rained

at bedtime, and all night the Oregon equivalents for the familiar English rats scrambled about the rafters and scratched on the loose shingles, and even burrowed their way in the loose hay under us. The rain soon cleared off, and some of us carried our blankets out into the field outside and finished out our sleep on the fresh-cut grass, perfumed by the recent rain.

The sun rose brilliantly, and we saddled early and were off, leaving behind us as quickly as we could the sluggard's settlement.

We soon slackened our pace, as after slowly climbing a wooded ridge the view of a lovely valley opened out.*

It was about six or seven miles long by three or four broad, encircled by gently sloping hills, wooded at the tops. Over their shoulders the more distant mountains on either side showed blue or snowy heads. A stream, as usual, flowed through the valley from end to end, fed every here and there by little brooks and runnels of clear water. The valley held four farms, the white houses in three cases shining out in the bright sun; the fourth farm was the first settler's, and was built of grey logs and shingles.

On the slope of the hill to the right stood the newest white house, and in front of it an inclosure of about half an acre, walled in with boards built up to five feet high, contained the first attempt at a vineyard and an orchard of young apple-tree, pears, and plums.

At the most distant farm at the farther end of the valley we pulled up to ask for a drink of water, and seeing two horsemen, the owner, in his white shirt-sleeves, came out to speak to us. He sent a small boy to the house for a jug and glasses, and then drew from the well in the flower-garden adjoining the house a fresh bucket full of the most sparkling and cool water, so cold that the cloud settled on the side of the tumbler as he filled it.

The gable end of the house was almost covered in roses and honeysuckle, which hung in sprays in front of the windows.

As the farmer stood talking to us a band of sheep, headed by a handsome white Angora goat, crowded round, and the goat came close and rubbed his close-curled head against his master's hand, regardless of the two deerhounds lying close by in the road, which had strolled out of the house to make our acquaintance.

The farmer said he liked the Angora goat with the sheep, he was so much more sensible than they; he kept them out of mischief, always brought them home at night, and would come whenever he was called.

We got off our horses and walked with the owner round the farm. He had been in Oregon sixteen years, having come from one of the western States. The first year he had hired himself out to work as a farm labourer at eighty cents a day. Then he hired a little farm on shares, the owner providing cattle and implements and seed, and taking half the produce. Then for three years he had rented a larger farm on similar terms, and at the end of that time he found he had 2,000 dollars. Then he bought a farm in the great Willamette valley, paying for it by degrees. Then after six years "traded" it for this farm among the hills, paying some 2,000 dollars to boot.

Now he owned 964 acres, of which 200 was cultivated and the rest was in grass for cattle and sheep. "And how many men have you besides yourselves to work this place?" we asked. One, was the answer. He went on—"I have got four good farm-horses,

weighing from 1,250 to 1,450 lb. each." "But how
do you manage with one man to keep this farm so
clean, and grow such crops?" (He had about fifty
acres of as good wheat as we ever saw, and the rest
of the 200 acres chiefly in oats.) "Well," said he,
"the seasons here are so regular that we go on putting in grain from November till April; last year
I sowed my last wheat on the 4th of May. When I
go to harrowing I lead one pair of horses and drive
the other; so you see we can cover a good many acres
in the day." "How many bushels of corn did you sell
last year?" "Last year I sold 2,300 bushels; this
year I expect to have 3,000 to sell." "What stock
have you?" "I have now got 100 horned stock,
200 sheep, and 100 Angora goats." "Do they have
any shelter and any dry food in the winter?" "They
lie out all the year round, but I give them a little
hay in the winter to help them." "Have you had
those goats long?" "Not more than three years. I
began with fifteen, of which eleven were ewes. The
fleeces average three pounds in weight, and the hair
sells for quite eighty-five cents a pound." "Then you
fancy these goats?" "Well, I do; they are less
trouble than sheep, quite as hardy, breed quite as

fast, and the hair is worth fully double the price of wool." "How far are you from a market?" "Not more than sixteen or seventeen miles, and it is a pretty good road: but I suppose we shall have that railway through before very long, sha'n't we, colonel?"

The man was worth that day probably more than 17,000 dollars, and had as sweet a home as farmer could wish, with prosperity following his energetic, healthy labour.

In Oregon the ladies take their share of public duties.

We made the acquaintance of a pretty, lively girl of five and twenty. A farmer's daughter, and educated at the Corvallis State Agricultural College,* she had passed most creditably through the classes there, and then went home to her father's house. There she kept the accounts and transacted the business of the farm, whilst she kept up her accomplishments, and was the life and soul of the household. The farmers round required a new secretary for their "Grange," or union. One suggested to another that Miss —— would do first rate. The idea took at once, and a unanimous invitation was shortly given to her that she should take the reins of office.

The idea, if pleasing, was bold; however, she assented. Now think of her in office, transacting the business and keeping the accounts of the grange.

This involves the affairs of perhaps thirty farms, whose owners make common sales and purchases of produce of all sorts; meet at stated times to discuss the price of wheat, the iniquities of the Grain-ring, the rise in freights, and the rest of the farmers' topics; they have storage in common for their corn, and a corporate life involving power to sue in common at law, and liability to be sued.

Never was the grange business better looked after than when the young lady secretary was in office.

The cares and duties of the secretaryship did not engross her entirely. A friend of ours went to visit her father in harvest-time. Our heroine's younger brother had fallen ill while driving the reaper. But she would not permit a check; so, jumping on the reaper, she drove the horses all that afternoon, and, as her father proudly said, did as good a day's work as any man on the place. Then she came in, presided at the supper-table, and afterwards played and sang all the evening.

It would be easy to multiply examples of the

several classes represented by the various experiences we have detailed.

But it seems that we have written enough to show the types of men we found in Oregon. Nearly all seemed pleased at the interest we took in their affairs, and answered freely, and we believe honestly and fairly, the questions we put.

CHAPTER IX.

To one brought up among the fixed habits, ancient institutions, and permanent ideas of the old country, it is very interesting to see a community which has just had a clean sheet on which to inscribe its laws, its religion, its public and private education, its social habits.

But it is difficult to convey in words the general impression left on the mind by reading many newspapers, consulting the codes of laws, the published constitutions of universities, colleges, and schools; talking with men in office, from the governor of the State to the peace officers in the country districts— the lawyers in the little towns, and the doctors, there as here, the hardest worked of professional men.

Although of course there are many rough customers about, disregard for and defiance of law seem very rare. Even in the wildest part the State's writ runs.

The marshal and his deputy go boldly and take a wrongdoer to trial and punishment without dispute or refusal, and a legal notice, posted on the court-house door, and advertised in the newspaper, sufficed to put a stop to illegal timber-cutting in the far recesses of the woods we passed through, or to maintain uninjured an objectionable turnpike-gate on a very retired road, which gate had been twice destroyed by the neighbouring farmers before its legality was established in court.

There *may* be a redeeming feature in the practice of electing judges by popular vote, and turning them out of office again every four years, which seems to an Englishman so utterly anomalous.

It *may* be that respect for the majesty of the law is inculcated by every village attorney, because he believes in his soul that next "fall" he will himself occupy the judge's seat, and claim as of right autho-rity and respect, and therefore pays that same respect to the judge whose successor he thinks he is to be. And the turbulent defendant subdues his angry passions at the "marshal's" bidding because he knows that if he can get his party to "run" him next October he will claim the same obedience himself.

But we found the wisest and best men almost of one opinion, that this frequent change of office lowered the standard of purity as well as of legal knowledge in the various ranks of judges. Again and again we heard great importance attached to an early change in this matter, which, by giving safety and permanence to judicial office, would raise the average of education, character, and position among those to whom the administration of justice was intrusted.

Thus, moreover, the first step would be made towards the formation of that upper class of educated men which seemed to us the one great want of the State. It is very hard for a judge to exhibit fearlessness and independence in his opinions when in a few short months the counsel whose arguments he is refusing to admit may sit in his place, and the parties to the suit, one of whom he is almost sure to displease, will form part of that public from which his future clients have to come.

If you look down the lists of university councils, school committees, church governments, and other ruling bodies of public institutions, you will find the "judges" well to the fore, and, if uninstructed, will

P

wonder whether there must not be as many courts
as suitors; but once a judge always a judge is the
rule, and the title once earned, by a four years' term,
is carried to the dying day.

The same necessity for pleasing popular opinion
runs through the public actions of these gentlemen
of whatever kind, and as they are, as a rule, clever,
active, and better educated than their storekeeping
and farming neighbours, they so frequently occupy
public positions of all kinds that there seems to an
independent looker-on to be great room for improvement in the decisions of those public bodies in which
their influence is felt.   Again and again is the
contrast apparent between the intelligence, honesty,
and effectiveness of the private actions of the
individual members of a corporation and the collec-
tive action of the whole body.   To us it seemed
that very much of this falling short in public affairs
was   attributable   to   the   impending   election   or
re-election,   and   the   necessity   each   man   felt   of
pleasing his party or his neighbours.

The fair side of this was the ambition, or at any
rate the readiness, to undertake public office shown
by many to whom the emoluments of office, or its

personal advantages, must have been perfectly
indifferent. Interest in the affairs, that is, the
politics, of the State, the county, the district, was
very generally shown.

Every little town has its four or five churches. Two
divisions of Methodists, the Presbyterians, Episcopa-
lians, and one or two kinds of Baptists, divide between
them by far the largest part of the religious members
of the community, whilst there are a few Roman
Catholics. Each congregation pays its own pastor or
teacher, has its own building, and deputes to its own
minister the sacred offices of baptizing, marrying, and
burying. The graveyards we did not notice as surrounding the churches; they appeared to be quiet
spots, chosen at some little distance from the towns
or villages.

The little local newspapers abound with personal
items. Not a child is born without the fact being
noted, and the editor's wish expressed for the mother's
speedy recovery. Not a wedding is celebrated without
a description, not limited to the number and dresses
of the bridesmaids, but descending to the particulars
of the dishes of the wedding supper, and praising the
excellence of the sauces and the lightness of the

pastry. Not a death is recorded without details of the illness, and mention of the doctor who attended.

We wondered how these little journals were supported.

The mystery was explained thus:—One day we were resting in the early hot afternoon under a wild cherry-tree near the roadside in the country leading down to Yaquina Bay, when we saw trudging along the dusty road a "respectably-dressed" young man. That is to say he had a white shirt, a black coat and waistcoat, and a soft, clerical-looking felt hat. He carried, slung from his shoulder, a small black valise. Seeing us lying on the grass he came near and sat down in the shade and talked. After answering a great many questions as to who we severally were, and what we were doing in that country, and so on, we proceeded to pump our friend in his turn. He told us that he was sub-editor of the *Corvallis Crucible*,* and that he was travelling to collect subscriptions and sell papers. His wallet was full of the week's issue, and he sold us two or three copies with great satisfaction.

We learned that he had nearly five hundred sub-scribers, scattered all over the district, and that every farmhouse took a copy. He seemed familiar with every detail of a newspaper, from the collection of "items," the reporting of a speech, or the writing of a leader, to the composing of the type, the pulling off the papers, and their folding and delivery.

When we were in Oregon political party spirit did not run very high, and we looked in vain for spicy epithets and venomous paragraphs.

The imputations by the "outs" on the "ins," that more clerks had been appointed than there were posts to fill, that the State contracts were jobbed, that the Capitol building was costing twice too much, that the printers were making their fortunes from the sums paid for printing and publishing the governor's annual message, and a few trifles of that sort, were no stronger than those one may read in the *Eatanswill Gazette*, or the *Eatanswill Independent* at home.

The medical profession seem not at all exclusive in Oregon, and nearly all practitioners advertise their various claims. Mrs. Mary Howell, M.D., for instance, states that her "office is over the drug store on Thirteenth Street, corner of Washington Street," that she may be consulted any day between ten and five, and that her specialities are female diseases; while in the next line you read that Professor Blackmore, M.D., a graduate of Bellevue College, New York, has come for a few months to give the Oregonians the benefit of his great experience and uniform success in consumption, rheumatism, and every other complaint, and that he will make no charge unless the patient is cured; whilst hydropathists, allopathists, homœopathists, and every other sort of "ists" offer their services. The Bob Sawyers and Ben Allens of Oregon are provided for in the medical department of the Willamette University at Salem, where sixty-three graduates have attained their M.D., and three have passed as Doctors of Pharmacy (Phar. D.)* Three years study of medicine, two full courses of lectures, a satisfactory thesis, and an approved examination are described as the "pre-requisites to graduation." Nine professors are engaged in the teaching of the medical students.

There are abundance of roads, wide stretches of clearing fifty to one hundred feet broad, where the trees have been cut down, and generally grubbed up; occasionally a stump projects eight or ten inches in the middle of the road. There is no broken stone and no gravel in common use. If extra care is given to the approach to a house, a few loads of loose stones are dredged from the bed of the nearest stream. In winter a few inches of mud make walking all but impossible away from the plank footpath of the streets; but every one has at least one horse and a buggy, and a great deal of visiting goes on.

In the towns one always sees a common hall or public-room. Through the winter there is a lecture, reading, singing, meeting, or some other entertainment almost every week, and to this the farmers and their families flock in from the neighbourhood.

In summer, neighbours meet for the picnic and camping-out parties, about which enough has already been said; and also they flock to each other's summonses for roof-raising, barn-building, bridge-laying, and other labours too great for the one or two pairs of hands which one family can command.

When a new settler has built his cabin and fenced in a few acres of adjacent land for his first year's crop, his next thought is for the one barn which answers for all the farm buildings seen about an English homestead.

He fells trees, and by degrees prepares the logs, cutting them as they lie, then splits them, and fits them for their places. Then he sends his boys out to tell his neighbours within, say six or seven miles radius, that he will raise his barn on Tuesday week. The wife sets to in good time, and roasts and bakes enough for a small army.

The day comes, and early after breakfast, say at eight o'clock, one waggon after another is seen nearing the farm, the man driving, his wife next him on the front seat, and behind on the other two cross seats sit the lads and the lasses. The horses are " unhitched," and the drag-chains put on, and soon from the woods the massive beams are dragged in towards the barn site with shouts and laughter.

Then all hands to the raising, and by dinner-time the frame is up, and the roof-tree and rafters in their places, leaving only the boarding to be nailed on at leisure to complete the barn. And so, work being done, the frolic begins in earnest. The piles of hot bread, and the fried and baked mutton, and the roast chickens and ducks disappear, followed by quantities of apple-pies, pumpkin-pies, stewed fruits, jams, cakes, cream, washed down with plenty of coffee. Then pipes and whisky and water appear, and singing and romping go on merrily till the—to these unsophisticated folk—terribly late hour of eight or nine o'clock; and then home they go, each prepared to render in turn the service he in turn receives.

A high value is set on education. Far away from towns, on farms miles away from a settlement, we met repeatedly brown-jacketed, high-booted, dirty-shirted, ragged-hatted fellows, who had ideas on the currency question, were familiar with American history, knew the wrongs and a few of the rights of the Alabama difficulty, and could talk intelligently on the labour question and Chinese immigration.

We asked one great ragged hobbledehoy, whom we met twenty miles away from the town, away out in the wilds, where he got his teaching. He replied with dignity, "I larned some time of the school-marm, who comes out all summer to the schoolhouse yonder; but next year I am going to attend college in to Corvallis."

College, we thought! His appearance was that of the shambling recruit one is used to see in the neighbourhood of Westminster. When we talked to the principal of that very college at Corvallis,* he told us that it was very common for the farmers to save and pinch to send their lads in to him for a couple of years, and that it was often a wonder to him to find

how much learning they had gathered up there in the
back country.

The college in question is a State institution, and
bears the grand name of "State Agricultural
College."

It has a large wooden building in the outskirts of
the town,* with a senior and a junior school, and an
arts and a physical side, the latter having been attended by ninety-five students in 1875-6. For its
endowment 90,000 acres of land have been set aside
by the United States Government. For the State
University at Eugene City, opened in 1876, 66,000
acres have also been provided, and for the public
schools in the State no less than 500,000 acres.

To constitute this last grand total, the sixteenth
and thirty-sixth sections of land of one square mile,
or 640 acres each in every township, are set apart.
The message of the Governor of the State for 1876
gives the following figures:—

Year 1875-6; persons in the State over four and
under twenty years of age, 48,473; number attending
public schools, 27,426; private schools, 3,441; no
schools, 13,143.

Though Oregon is so young a State, there are the

insane to be provided for. A public hospital in East Portland* has been constituted by law, in which 337 patients were treated between September, 1874, and September, 1876. Of these 85 had been discharged as cured, 33 had died in the two years, and 218 remained under treatment on the 1st September, 1876. But Oregon must not lie under the stigma of furnishing the patients, since of the 218 above referred to, 30 were immigrants from Missouri, 14 from Illinois, 12 each from New York and Indiana, and smaller numbers from fifteen other States: whilst of the 76 of foreign birth 26 were born in Ireland and 13 in Germany, England only being charged with 6.

The State Penitentiary is at Salem, where 104 prisoners were confined on the 1st September, 1876. From the Report to the Legislature by the Superintendent of the Penitentiary, we gather that he returns the annual cost to the State of each convict as 175 dollars 14 cents, or about 25*l.* The experiment is being tried of leasing out the convicts to labour at various trades, and a certain number are working in blacksmiths' shops, tanneries, boot and shoe factories, and brickyards, at wages returning to the State 50 cents, or 2*s.* a day for each man.

The State has also formed an Institute for the Blind, where nine pupils were being taught in 1876, at the expense of the community; the institute being considered as part of the common-school system. The deaf and dumb also are not neglected. The State has provided an asylum where twenty-six inmates were received and cared for during the years 1875 and 1876.

The Capitol buildings of the State are erected at Salem, a town on the Willamette River, about a hundred miles[*] from Portland. They stand on a very fine site above the town, the front of the building facing westwards towards the coast range and the ocean; while the back windows command a lovely prospect of the Cascade Mountains, the snow-capped Mount Jefferson being in full view.

The design is very imposing, and has reference more to the future than to the present needs of the State. It is but partly finished, though 201,728 dollars, or more than 40,000l. had been expended on it up to September, 1876. The part completed gives accommodation to the Governor and other State officers, to the Senate, to the United States Supreme Court, and to the State Library. This last contains books of reference, both legal and general, and in point of completeness and arrangement is most creditable to the officials in charge.　In one of the corridors is preserved as a relic, and shown with pride, the first printing-press in the State, a somewhat significant emblem of what the young State prizes most.

If we have written a dull chapter, the reader must forgive us.　What after all can be but an imperfect sketch, would have been yet more incomplete without giving an idea of the point of social development already attained ; not a bad result, we venture to think, of only thirty years efforts at founding and promoting the institutions common throughout the world to civilised life.

CHAPTER X.

WE travelled northwards by train from Albany to Salem, the State Capitol just described. There we were introduced to Governor Chadwick,[*] and by him courteously received. He took us over the Capitol building, showing us the library, Senate chamber, and so on.

From the front of the building we looked over the houses and factories of the town of Salem, bordering the Willamette River for some distance, and across a wide stretch of open country to the distant coast range. The open land is in Yamhill County, which the Governor described as likely before many years to rival in wheat-growing the other counties lower down the valley.

We passed north again towards Oregon City. The great valley contracted its boundaries, the lower hills of the Cascades pushing their spurs forwards, covered with lines of firs; the river banks grew higher and more broken, and stone and rocks became visible by degrees.

The distinctive features of verdure and richness of vegetation which had marked our journey from the extreme southern boundary of the State passed away, and the train ran into the Oregon City station, the town lying on the lower level between the railway line and the river, and the rocks towering for several hundred feet above on the right.

This town bids fair to be the chief manufacturing centre of the State.* The broad Willamette falls over a ridge of rocks, with a height of over fifty feet, just above the town, and gives abundant water-power for factories and mills without end.

The situation has been seized for various purposes already. On the railroad, or eastern bank of the river, stand in succession sawmills, a woollen factory, flour-mills, machine-shops.

On the western side is the ship canal, cut in the grey rock, and giving access for the stern-wheel steamers to the Upper River, and enabling the freights of grain and wool and other agricultural products to be carried by water, without transhipment, from far up the valley to Portland, where the ocean-going ships lie to load.

We climbed to the top of the hill overhanging the town, and looked for miles up the stretch of the broad river above the falls.

In the distance the water was a pale grey colour, changing gradually into a clear green as it approached its leap. At the falls the river was contracted, and the dark line of the timber staging of the lumber-mill divided off the green from the white water for some distance. In the middle of the main fall a dark rock showed its head, and then a wide line of water, white and foaming, led the eye to another dark rocky island, above which was the grey wall of the ship canal.

From the height, whence we looked down, the sound of the waterfall was hardly audible, and the sense of motion, rush and change, inseparable from the near presence of such an object, was lost entirely in the calm and stillness of the sunny sky and gentle breeze. The red roofs of the town below shone in the sun, and a good many chimneys showed themselves against the water-line.

The hills near the town are full of iron ore. A large smelting-works and foundry have been established for a few years, the deposits of ore yielding about fifty-four per cent. of iron. The woollen mills employ over a hundred work-people, more than half of whom are Chinese. The goods from this factory were exhibited at the Centennial Exhibition, and received medals and diplomas, the fancy cassimeres and blankets being specially commended.

Near this place too is a paper-mill, producing about 2,000 lb. of paper daily.*

At Oregon City, and also at Salem, Albany, and McMinville, dried fruit works are in operation, where, under the process known as the "Alden," plums, pears, apples, strawberries, and smaller fruits are preserved and canned for the Eastern and European markets.

At Oregon City, one of the five United States Land Registrars for the State of Oregon has his office. There can be seen the survey maps of the neighbouring counties, townships, and sections, and the nature of every acre of surveyed land is shown.

As very mistaken notions prevail in England as to the land laws in the United States, it may be useful to any reader, who seeks information here to guide his actions to summarise very shortly the real position.

Q

In the year 1850 the Congress of the United States passed what is called the " donation law," under which those who had immigrated or would immigrate to Oregon before the 1st of December, 1850, would receive the following grants from the public land, namely, for a married couple, a whole mile section of 640 acres; for a single man, half that quantity. After the date named the grants were limited to half these acreages. The lands comprised in these donation grants are some of the very best in the State, for the early tide of settlement followed up the great Willamette Valley, and the level, easily-tilled bottom-lands were the first picked out. Many of such farms are now worth from 40 dollars to 60 dollars, or from 10*l.* to 12*l.* per acre.

The grants to the great railroad and waggonroad corporations in the State extend to the alternate or odd-numbered sections of one square mile, or 640 acres within a belt, having the railroad or waggon-road for its centre line, and extending from twenty miles on either side of the railroad, to six miles on either side of the waggonroad.

The other, even-numbered, sections of land remain the property of the United States Government, and are subject to the operation of the homestead or pre-emption laws.

Under the " homestead " law every head of a family, male or female, and every single man over twenty-one years of age, being either citizens of the United States, or having declared their intention of becoming such, can, on payment of the land-office fees of from 7 dollars to 22 dollars, enter on any eighty acres of the public lands within the limits of the railroad or waggonroad grants, or on any 160 acres of public land outside such limits.   The settler can obtain, as of right, a government title to such land on fulfilling the conditions of five years' residence on the land, and the expenditure of 300 dollars or 60*l.* in improvements.

Mineral lands, bearing gold, silver, cinnabar, or copper, are excluded from the operation both of the homestead and pre-emption laws, and are subject to the special legislation affecting mining claims.

Under the " pre-emption " law the qualifications of the claimant are the same as under the homestead acts; but, in addition, he must not be in possession of a half-section or 320 acres in any of the states or territories of the United States.   The pre-emption

rights are that on payment, at a United States land
office, of an entering fee of 2 dollars, such a qualified
claimant may choose 160 acres, or a quarter-section,
either within or outside the limits of a railroad or
waggonroad grant, paying for the government land in
the first case 2 dollars 50 cents per acre, and in the
latter case 1 dollar 25 cents per acre.

But by this time it is difficult to find very desirable
portions of government land within the limits of
distance from a road, on which to establish a home
under the acts above referred to, and the railroad
and waggonroad corporations are practically the
sources of supply of unimproved or virgin land.

Very favourable terms are offered by these large
owners to settlers who purchase from them.

But a good deal, not only of courage, but of experience of the stern necessities of wild life ought
to be the portion of the newly-arrived settler who
ventures on to unimproved land. His capital is being
absorbed before his eyes in house-building, fencing,
clearing, ploughing, as well as in the household
necessaries of the first and second years.

The only exception is in any case where special
facilities are or may be given by any of the land-

owning corporations to newly-arriving immigrants. If
such an one has been able to arrange, not only for
payment for his land by gradual instalments, but also
for being furnished by the corporation, directly or
through their credit and influence, with help towards
his necessary outgoings, then, and only then, ought he
to venture on to what is properly and expressively
called "wild" land.

It is true that if the settler makes up his mind to
take such a risk, the kindly climate and rich soil
may fairly be expected to secure him against loss of
crops or of stock from inclemency of weather or
poverty of land. And he will have the satisfaction
afterwards of reaping all the fruits of his patience
and labour.

But our advice to any seeking a home in Oregon
is first to choose by careful inquiry and actual in-
spection the district for his settlement in accordance
with his own powers and tastes; then, if he can, let
him hire himself out for twelve months as a farm
help, secure of gaining good wages, as well as
invaluable experience, and let him deposit his
capital at interest of ten or twelve per cent. in

a safe bank, or on mortgage through a respectable lawyer.

Or he may, if he has already a sufficient knowledge of a farmer's life and work, hire a farm on shares. The owner of the land will receive a third of the produce if the settler provides implements, seed, farming-stock, and labour; or probably one half if these necessaries are found by the owner himself.

The newcomer will, in this case, be able to depend on a considerable increase to his capital by the end of the first or second year, and then he may, with prudence, become a landowner himself, with the certainty, that having bought at existing prices, his land will increase in value year by year, and his own position undoubtedly improve, while his children will have open to them the various careers afforded by the agricultural, manufacturing, commercial, or professional openings in this growing State.

The questions are often asked if it is safe to employ British capital in Oregon, and if foreigners do not lie under disadvantages as compared with American citizen.

The constitution of the State provides as follows :—
" Foreigners who are or may hereafter become
residents of this State shall enjoy the same rights
in respect to the possession, enjoyment, and descent
of property, as native-born citizens." And further :
"Any alien, or non-resident citizen of the United
States, may acquire and hold lands, or any right
thereto or interest therein, by purchase, devise, or
descent ; and he may convey, mortgage, and devise
the same ; and, if he shall die intestate, the same
shall descend to his heirs ; and, in all cases such
lands shall be held, conveyed, mortgaged, or devised,
or shall descend in like manner, and with like effect,
as if such alien were a native or citizen of this
State."

A married woman may hold, in her own right,
property of every description possessed at the time
of her marriage, or acquired afterwards by gift, devise,
or inheritance, which property is exempt from liability for the debts or contracts of the husband. The
same exemption applies to real or personal property
acquired by married women through their own labour.

Taxation in Oregon is very light. A poll-tax of

one dollar is levied on every adult inhabitant. State taxes for 1874 amounted to five and a half mills, the county taxes ranged from five to twelve mills, and school taxes averaged three mills in the dollar of value of real and personal property assessed for taxation.

CHAPTER XI.

IN order properly to appreciate the life and bustle of an American town of sixteen or seventeen thousand inhabitants, it is necessary to have been travelling for a month or two previously through the country.

Portland seemed to us to be nearly as great a place as San Francisco. The approach to it is of the same kind, in so far as that the railway lands us on the eastern side of the Willamette, and that a big ferry-boat transfers us across the river to the city.

The city rises from the water's edge, and covers what used to be pine-clad hills. The depth of water allows the grain-ships to lie alongside the wharves to load, and there is a busy scene with the river steamboats and tugs and ferry-boats passing and repassing. The original wooden shanties are being rapidly replaced with great structures of stone and brick. Warehouses are full of grain, wool, skins, canned salmon, and meat; logs and planks of pine and cedar are stacked in high piles. Several church spires, and the court-house, theatre, and custom-house show prominently above the mass of roofs.

We arrived about eight o'clock in the evening, and went straight to the Metropolitan Hotel. The host asked if we would mind having sleeping-rooms at a house of his on the other side of the street, as the hotel was full. We unpacked and dined, and then went to the theatre.

It was the benefit of the star of a troupe of travelling actors from San Francisco. The pretty house looked bare with an audience of only about fifty people; and the two acts of *Othello* and one from the *Lady of Lyons* fell flat compared with the half-hour of screaming farce which concluded the performance. We went home to supper, and then to bed, our rooms being at the back of the building. About two in the morning we were woke by the loud, persistent clanging of a bell. The jalousies were closed, and the moon shone brightly through the chinks. But a red glare lighted up the chim-

neys of buildings behind, which rose above the line
of roofs of the houses, one of which we were
occupying.

We got up and looked out, dressed hastily, and
ran down stairs, though it was a few moments before
our scattered wits divined the danger. The crowd
had already gathered in the street below, and one
after another we heard the fire-engines rushing up.
By the time the door was opened, the hotel on the
other side of the street, in which we had tried to
get rooms, was in one blaze. As we looked, the
flames crept quickly along the wooden cornice
below the roof of the hotel; and almost as quickly
as the words can be written, the upper stories of
the four shops adjoining were on fire.

The crowd by this time had filled the street, and
five fire-engines were pouring volumes of water on
to the burning block. The volunteer firemen in
uniform acted as officers to a wild mass of men,
who dragged about the hose, broke open the doors
and windows of the burning houses, set ladders in
their places, emptied the rooms of their furniture
and the stores below of their goods, fixed great iron
hooks on to the standards of the burning verandahs,

and tore them away from their places to keep the fire from spreading.

Fortunately there was but little wind. The new buildings of a newspaper-office, within a few feet of the blazing hotel, but separated by a narrow wharf leading to the river in the rear, being saturated and deluged with water, did not catch. And next the other end of the burning block stood a little one-storied Chinese washerman's house, which we had remarked on the evening before as an unsightly gap in the lofty street front.

This saved the town. The firemen could thus get to direct their hose full on to the side and back of the end house which was blazing. In an hour-and-a-half the roofs fell in, carrying with them the whole fronts of the buildings into the furnace within; a great mass of flame shot up into the moonlit sky, followed by a dense white cloud of smoke, and the danger to the adjoining and opposite houses was over.

One poor fellow lost his life. He had come in late with two friends, all somewhat the worse for drink. When the alarm was given, the landlord rushed round the house, opening and breaking in

every bedroom door. The unfortunate guest was
shaken out of his heavy sleep, but the man who
called him passed on perforce to the adjoining
rooms to rouse their occupants: the drunken man
must have sunk back to sleep, or have failed to
realise his instant danger, and he was never seen
again alive.

After an hour or two's rest we looked out again.

Where the hotel and shops had stood the evening
before, there was but an unsightly black ruin. We
thought thankfully of the escape we had had.*

We walked through the main streets of the town,
and admired the well-filled shops, the broad streets,
the houses of the residents, set some little way back
from the road, with a little garden to each, filled
with flowering-shrubs and flowers.

We climbed to the top of the hill behind, and
looked over the town to the broad river, with the
shipping dotting its surface, the masts and rigging
standing out clear in the bright, sunny air; while
away, farther to the east, the snowy summit of Mount
Hood towered up eleven thousand feet into the sky.

The next evening we sailed, on our return to
San Francisco and home.

The *City of Chester*, the shortest steamship for her height out of the water, and almost the slowest that ever was built, was lying alongside the wharf, and we sailed about ten in the evening. The moon was high in the heavens, and nearly full, as we gently moved off into the stream, and the snowy Mount Hood shone out, and his lesser brethren loomed darkly in the distance.

The immediate banks of the Willamette, between Portland and the point where it falls into the great Columbia, are comparatively flat and tame. Wide, rich pastures close by, and luxuriant grain fields behind, lead the eye across them to the mighty range behind; and as we passed by, the white night-fog lay in wreaths.

We turned into our berths late, and got up early, to find that we had entered the Columbia. The general type of scenery reminded us of the Sogne Fjord in Norway, except that the mountains were not so rugged; but the river was so vast, that one insensibly thought of it as an arm of the sea, and expected a salt taste when the spray dashed up once or twice into our faces.

There was a large ship's company. One or two

Portland folk with their wives were going down to visit their " Canneries " at various points on the river. Others were Italian fishermen, of whom nearly 400 are engaged in these salmon-fisheries; four or five pilots were on board, whose boats were lying off the Columbia Bar; several of the passengers were San Francisco or Eastern commercial travellers, returning from their rounds in Oregon, with the agricultural machinery, sewing-machines, pianos, and patent medicines, which are the modern substitutes for the wooden nutmegs and Yankee clocks of our old friend Sam Slick.

In an hour or two's time we drew towards the bank. The shore was rocky and steep, and covered with thick scrub, from which the pine-trees rose high in the air. A curious structure stood some distance out into the stream, built on piles, under which the river flowed freely. Long, low-boarded sheds, covered with red shingles, and a more substantial and higher building, with tall chimneys in the centre, all built on these piles, formed the " Cannery."

A white house with garden in front under the cliff, and a row of workmen's houses at the side, completed the establishment. Quite a fleet of open boats, each

fitted for a pair of oars, but provided with mast and
sail, lay moored to the piles, and the nets were hanging
out to dry, or piled in heaps in the boats. There
stood a great stack of white deal cases, each about
fourteen inches square, on the wharf in front of the
sheds, and some twenty Chinamen came clustering
through the wide central doors as the steamer came
neatly alongside, and was moored ready to receive
cargo.

The door in the ship's side was opened, planks
laid down, and the Chinamen began their labours.
Each seized one of the deal cases and slid it down
into the hold, and moved so methodically, and quickly
too, that it took only an hour and a half or thereabouts to ship 1,300 cases.

The owner of this first cannery was on board, and
very kindly took us over it.

We passed through two or three of the dark-boarded
sheds, till we came to the farthest, the floor of which
was covered with the salmon caught the night before.
Only 240 fish lay there; but the season was drawing
to a close on the 5th of August, and another fortnight
would finish it. It opens on the 20th of April.
Earlier in the season the catch ranged from 1,000 to

1,750 fish. The average weight was about twenty-eight pounds, and we saw no fish over thirty-five. We did not admire them very much ; they were short and thick, and rather clumsy-looking, with a good deal of head, and a strong tinge of red down to the shoulders.

The process of canning is very simple. The fish are cut with great fixed knives into pieces the length of the tin can. Then, being packed closely into the tin, the top is soldered down. The tin is put into a boiler, with many others, and boiled for an hour and a half in water at 212 degrees. When this first boiling is over, a man stabs the top of each tin with a sharp awl, and so lets out the steam. The hole so made is directly soldered over again, and the tins are boiled for two hours in salt water at a temperature of 230 degrees. The canning process is then complete, and all that remains is to set the cans to cool, to label them, and pack them in boxes for shipment.

The can-making is a very pretty craft ; one good hand, whom we saw at work, can solder 1,500 tins a day, the materials being set ready to his hand.

The neat deal boxes are made in Portland. Each case holds four dozen boxes of one pound weight, and is sold for about six dollars a case.

R

This cannery, which was one of the largest, can clean, cook, tin, and pack ready for shipment from twelve hundred to fifteen hundred fish a day.

The fishermen are not the servants of the "cannery," but work for the establishment on a somewhat singular plan.

The boats and seines are the property of the cannery, and are let out to the fishermen in consideration of one-third of the catch of fish. The other two-thirds belong to the fisherman for his labour and skill, but he has to sell them to the cannery for fifty cents a fish.

These men make very large sums in a good season; but the business, like many others, consisting of a short spell of long hours of work, and then months of idleness, is really healthy neither for mind nor body; and, as a rule, the fishermen, after a few seasons, either go once more to sea, or return to their native Italy, or settle down in Oregon on the land.

This last year or so the catches of salmon have not been so large. Perhaps it is that sixteen or seventeen of these "canneries," each accounting for some 80,000 fish in the season, have made a diminution even in the vast supplies of the Columbia; perhaps salmon, like so many other creatures of flood and field, go and come in varying numbers in periods measured by tens or twenties of years. It is certain that the fishermen have found the common tracks of the fish near the shores on either side, and set their nets in the direct road of the ascending multitudes.

We hope that before irreparable damage has been done to these fisheries, proper precautions may be taken to give the salmon their Sunday free, even though a police regulation to that effect might be difficult to enforce.

The magnitude of the salmon-fishery may be judged from the fact that 428,730 cases, of the aggregate value of 2,329,000 dollars, were exported in 1876.

Some of the more far-seeing owners of the canneries are devoting their attention to canning beef and mutton as well, taking up this when the salmon season is over.

The quantity of canned beef exported in 1876 amounted to 33,250 cases, valued, with what was pickled and sent out in cases and barrels, at 350,000 dollars.

In the course of the same afternoon we reached Astoria, planted within the great Columbia River bar.

The sun shone brightly on the white houses dotted about on the hill-sides, and grouped among the pine-trees.

The slope of the hills behind is so steep as to afford no room for the rapidly-growing town, and piles are being pushed far out into the water, on which rows of houses and shops are built.* But American enterprise is hard at work; and already a broad gap in the sky-line behind shows where a road is cut through, the displaced rock and stone being run in waggons rapidly down the steep slope and tilted into the margin of the river. Firm foundations are thus gained, and before long a solid line of wharves, lined with substantial warehouses, will accommodate the extending trade.

Several large ships were lying at anchor, and the little town was full of life and bustle.

Our steamer took in another large consignment of tinned salmon, which brought her head down another foot into the water, and somewhat improved her appearance. But we were not mistaken in foreboding a tremendous tossing as we breasted the bar over which the long rollers from the Pacific were showing their white crests.

We made very little way in face of wind and tide, and we looked back regretfully on the easy motions of the *Germanic* as we pitched and rolled.

The bar is one constantly shifting and changing. The northern channel is pretty nearly closed to shipping, which now crowds along the southern shore.

The sailors foretell that ere long the great river will once again break through the barrier and resume its former outflow, and that this southern channel will give place to the northerly passage. It is high treason at Portland to hint that this great bar is in any sense a barrier to trade ; but we heard of several instances of sailing ships, and steamers too, being detained in winter time for many days, unable to get in or out.

We heard also of commercial troubles from delays in delivery of cargoes so caused.

We may be permitted, therefore, to hope that, before many years are past, the contemplated outlay on the Yaquina port may be made by the United States Government, and that passengers and produce from or to the interior of the State may be saved a couple of hundred miles in distance and a couple of days in time in the journey out from, or into the Willamette valley from San Francisco or the East.

Recent newspapers tell us that there has been duly voted by Congress the appropriation of three million dollars for the improvement of some port and the creation of a harbour of refuge on the Pacific coast.

We hope that the superior claims of Yaquina Bay will command attention: certainly there appears no other port between San Francisco and the Columbia offering at once shelter of a bold headland from the north-west gales; a natural reef of rocks protecting the entrance, but showing a safe run-in both north and south; a land-locked bay inside, with a deep water-channel extending eight or ten miles up with an average width of nearly half a mile. Add to these advantages that there is easy access to the interior country through a wide opening in the coast range, which almost everywhere else bars the coast from the great valley.

The railway now in progress from Corvallis in the valley westwards to the bay must not be forgotten in the array of the facilities given by the various ports.

We steamed slowly along the coast, some four or five miles out, with a calm sea, a white fog-bank lying to the west, and the sun hardly shining through the thin veil of clouds overhead.

The whole distance we saw from time to time the white summits of the Cascades showing over the sombre outlines of the pine-clad*coast range, and as night drew on and the distant view faded away, we bade farewell to Oregon.

CHAPTER XII.

WHEN we looked out the next morning we were running along the coast of California. What a contrast! High white cliffs, in long, straight stretches, unbroken by the coves and combes and woods of Oregon—the sea rolling in against the narrow beach, with hardly any shore—an inhospitable - looking country.

In one or two of the indentations of the downs on the higher level little towns and clusters of houses nestled, with open roadsteads in front, in which here and there a coasting schooner was moored.

The captain told us that when a north-west breeze rises it freshens rapidly into a gale. There is no shelter, no harbour of refuge along all this coast, and the schooners caught in such a case anchor, the crews batten all tightly down and betake themselves on shore and watch their vessel, trusting to the strength

her cables to hold her from drifting in. Generally
the vessel escapes : sometimes she is driven bodily
shore and blown high on to the beach, where her
timbers lie for years.

A considerable trade is done between San Francisco
and these little coast towns in lumber, corn, wool, and
other agricultural and pastoral produce.

As we passed along southwards the prevailing
colour of the coast changed, and reds and browns
varied the white cliffs. The ships became more
numerous, all flocking towards the same point. The
rocks showed broken and rugged in the hot bright
sun, and on every point sat a gull, or albatross,
whole families of which followed us for many miles,
circling in numbers round the ship and swooping
down on the scraps of broken meats thrown out to
them from time to time. Ridges of rocks pushed
out into the sea, with here and there a sunken one
over which the waves broke heavily.

Then a wide gap gradually opened in the coastline.
The ship turned sharply in, and we passed through
the Golden Gate, the splendid stretch of calm water
within bathed in sunlight. The hills on either
hand almost merit the name of mountains : in form

they are very like those of Mid Wales. They are
covered with masses of brown heather and dark green
gorse. Hardly one stunted tree is seen, except where
a white house has been built and fruit-trees planted.

Here and there a seal or sea-lion shows his round,
black head, and everywhere the white gulls and grey
albatrosses seem at home.

We neared the city, passing along its sea face with
its long line of docks and wharves. Huge piles of
wheat in bags lay everywhere ready for shipment
to Europe and the East.

We found the whole city in a condition of suppressed
excitement. The night but one before the riots had
broken out, and the loafers and "hoodleums" for a
few hours had held mad revel in the streets.

The railway riots in the East had given a pretext,
but the mob in San Francisco had tried to set the
city on fire in several places, but had failed, even in
the case of the Pacific Steamship Company, whose
wharves and dock had been several times assailed.
They had then burst into China Town and had
wrecked several houses, had broken a great many
windows, and maltreated the blue-frocked, long-tailed
inmates whenever they could get hold of them.

A good many fears had been felt, as the police force was unable to cope with such an army of ruffianism. But the public spirit of the well-to-do inhabitants was at once invoked.

The survivors of the Vigilance Committee of 1849 had met at the City Hall. The Mayor had sworn them in as special constables, and they had summoned their friends to their side, and in a very few hours some 6,000 friends of order were enrolled. These were divided into companies of 100 each, and patrolled the city, each man armed with club and revolver.

The mob had never ventured to try conclusions, but after a few spasmodic attempts had given in, and were chased from the streets whenever they showed a head. And the following night, that preceding our arrival, the city was quiet. We turned out for a walk after dinner, and were out till midnight; but were not rewarded by seeing even one single fight, and the streets were as quiet and calm as those of London itself. We passed a few pleasant days, accepting as far as possible the kindly hospitality showered on us from all sides.

One of our hosts lived out an hour and a half from

the city, southwards, at a place called Menlow Park. As we write the name, the scene again is present before us.

We are in a long car again, with all the blinds drawn down the windows on the side on which the sun is glaring: the red plush of the cushions looks as hot as it feels to the touch. A good deal of white dust eddies in at the open door at the farther end. The car is well filled, a number of the rich citizens returning after a very short day's work at their offices, their wives and daughters, in cool muslin or holland dresses and light veils, taking home their purchases.

The train stops, and the carriage is nearly emptied of its occupants. Six or seven buggies, each with its pair of nervous-looking, highly-bred horses, are waiting, the only thing slovenly about the equipages to an English eye being, as a rule, the liveries, or want of liveries, of the coachmen.

The whole of the neighbouring land is quite flat, and the eye catches sight of long vistas of broad, grey, dusty roads, between covers of thick bush of evergreen oak, poison oak, with brilliant red and yellow leaves, dusty blackberry bines, and the

common oak-trees stretching wide branches over
the scrub, each almost meeting his next neighbour.

The roads from the station are lined with neat,
white palings, instead of the usual log fence. We
have scarcely driven three minutes time from the
station, when there is a sudden change. The brush
has all been grubbed up, three out of four of the
oak-trees have disappeared, and there is a stretch
of emerald-green turf, dotted with lovely deodoras,
pines, cedars, eucalyptus, and pampas-grass, mixed
with a variety of flowering-shrubs.

In the middle of a large compound there is a
blaze of scarlet flowers, and behind, almost hidden
by the trees and shrubs, stands the house, a long,
low structure, festooned in clematis, honeysuckle,
and roses, with a deep, shady verandah round three
sides — wide, overhanging eaves, and the upper
windows closed with dark-green jalousies.

The blue green of the eucalyptus mixes with the
various shades of the conifers, and the eye ranges
over plants one would be glad of under glass here.
The mystery of freshness is explained as we drive
up to the door.

On the grass there is trailing a flexible hose,

attached to a curious spindly iron stand, from the top of which radiate crosswise four arms, rotating horizontally, each sending a fine shower of water some eight or ten feet, and sprinkling as it turns. As we look, a Chinese gardener, with broad-brimmed straw hat, appears, and drags the apparatus a few feet further on the lawn, and so, in default of natural, an artificial rain is kept constantly at work.

Cost is the only drawback ; the water for a garden will cost from three to six hundred dollars a year. But that is of the least consequence to these folk ; no poor man can live there at all, and when a man is rich in San Francisco, he *is* rich, and spares no money to surround himself and his family with all the luxuries that coin can buy.

The State fair was just open in San Francisco ere we left. Whatever one would look for in a similar exhibition at home was displayed, from steam-engines to mousetraps, sewing-machines to beehives, telescopes to knife-grinders ; all sorts of mechanical contrivances were seen. Corn of all sorts ; fruits and flowers, wines, oil, silk ; various metals and ores. Art-needlework, and embroidery, pictures, pianofortes, furniture in

lovely woods, polished and inlaid; various chemical
products, tinned meats and fish.

Meanwhile a large band of wind and stringed
instruments were in full force, and most creditably
they played; the large building was crammed with
visitors.   We roamed here and there, finding it hard
indeed to credit that what we saw in its raw material,
and its manufactured condition, was nearly all the
product of that single State, and that the work had
really all been done since 1850, that is in seven and
twenty years.   No wonder its natives are proud of the
Golden State, and foresee a splendid future for the
Pacific slope.

Our friends besought us to arrange to pass a winter
there.   The same clothing, except a slightly thicker
great coat for morning and evening wear, is carried
as in summer.   The sun at midday is not so hot,
but again they say the forenoon wind is not so strong
and driving.   Travelled Californians will always tell
you that they have no inducement to leave home, at
any time of the year, for change of climate, and
wherever they go, they say, with apparent earnest-
ness, "There's no place like home."

But lanky forms, pale faces, bright eyes, quick,

active movements, and hasty tempers tell their own tale of life at high pressure, men kept in constant training; the race has many markedly admirable characteristics; but there is no denying that living so fast, they cannot live so healthily and so long as residents of a more temperate and cooler clime, with fewer fluctuations of success and failure.

We make no scruple of avowing our strong preference for Oregon, and our belief in its more solid if not so rapidly-growing prosperity.

CHAPTER XIII.

THE climb back to the top of the Sierra Nevada, returning eastwards, seems steeper than the westward descent. The engines labour and tug and strain, while the hot sun beats fiercely on the carriage tops, and we all sit panting in our shirt-sleeves, or light dust coats, praying for the cool evening breezes.

We intended staying at Salt Lake, to pay our respects to Brigham Young ; but when we got to Ogden Junction, we heard of his serious illness, and in a day or two, of his death.* The easy way in which the reins of power he dropped were picked up by the college of apostles (of cardinals we were going to say) was a surprise to many besides ourselves. One heard everywhere that a general disruption of the church, or vast changes in its constitution at least, must follow the sudden departure of so masterful a leader, who had been so thoroughly the author and architect of the

S

success (so far as it succeeded) of the Mormon organisation.

But no change of policy has yet appeared. People said that a great inroad of Gentiles would be made; that a mixed population would hold the land; and that the Mormon church would have to move its headquarters once again, if its peculiar features were to be upheld.

But they had not taken account of the foresight of the leader who had gone to his account.

There are but few watercourses in the country, and in Utah fertility, even the necessaries of life themselves, depend on access to these streams. These rivers and water powers are all owned and held by the Mormon settlers, and Gentile immigrants found themselves at the mercy of these men. Land they might have, but no water. The victory of the general features of the vigorous American life over the peculiar customs and degrading institutions of the Mormon church will depend, it seems to us, on whether the attraction of the mineral wealth of the country can overcome the resistance of the present owners to the residence among them of the Gentile miners.

Outside its mines Utah offers few attractions to the settler, to whom in other States such infinitely greater advantages in soil, climate, and free social life lie open.

As we passed along in the train over the prairies, there were herds of innumerable cattle being driven eastwards. We counted up to several hundreds in one drove, and estimated it to consist of at least five thousand head. They had doubtless been collected in those splendid pastures of Oregon that we had seen, and having journeyed through the spring and summer months, would now very shortly come to the end of their free quarters, and be packed closely in the railway trucks and shipped away east. Some would be slaughtered at Chicago, others in the Eastern States, and some would find their way to English markets.

We changed our route at Omaha, and travelled to Chicago over the Burlington and Quincy road; struck always by the unbroken line of farms, varied with prosperous towns and villages, everything growing, full of life.

Surely no English traveller can pass, with open eyes, from one side to the other of this vast continent, without having forced on him the tremendous contrast between the narrow, monotonous lives of so many thousands of his fellow-countrymen and their struggle for existence, with the sense of freedom, of opportunity, of prosperity of the settler in the West.

It is difficult to repress a sigh of envy at the broad, fertile lands of these newly-settled States. One can sympathise with the suggestion of the Western man, who was travelling towards England, but hoped that when he got to Liverpool and went to London, the train might keep the rails, lest she should run off into the sea on either side; and who supposed that in England one was never out of sight of the waves.

From Chicago, eastwards, we took the Michigan central route, leading us by Detroit and Niagara. The railroad runs for some miles along the south-eastern shore of Lake Michigan.

The day was stormy and the wind rough; the brown waves came curling in on the beach with white tops of a thoroughly orthodox fashion. Of course no land whatever was visible across the lake, water and sky met in the horizon; the ships were rising and falling at their anchors; one or two steam-tugs were puffing about in the usual restless, undefined way; sailors in proper costume were loitering in little knots on the wharves, hands in their pockets, quids in their mouths; a fresh smell was in the wind.

Could this great expanse of water be anything but the sea? The longer the train ran in full sight, the harder it became to believe in one's map, and refuse the evidence of one's eyes. But this map showed a group of four of these great lakes, and this Lake Michigan not the largest. We tried, but failed, to imagine clearly the volume, the acreage of water.

Previous experience of lakes at home and abroad gave no guide; Lake Windermere, Lake Leman, Lake of Como, Lake Mjösen, Bandag's Vaud, each in turn was brought into comparison; but the mountains surrounding each, the opposite shore visible if distant, the inflowing rivers, the little ships and trim boats: all impressed on the mind the sense of "the piece of water surrounded by land." Here none of these essentials of a lake were present to the eye; we were indeed coasting along an inland sea.

In passing, a word of gratitude may be forgiven us for the comforts and ease of the Pullman cars on this road, and the excellence and cheapness of the travelling hotel car, where all our meals were served.

The rest of that afternoon and evening we were crossing the State of Michigan, which does not show to the passing traveller many more signs of advanced civilisation than Iowa and Nebraska; one sees thick woods from which the tilled ground has been re-claimed; rough farming; a good deal of water standing about in the low grounds; while the cornfields exhibit a rich undergrowth of weeds.

Towards midnight we drew near Detroit, where we were to pass once again under the rule of Her Majesty the Queen. The moon shone very brightly as the train moved slowly on to a huge ferry-boat, and was there made fast. The river flowed calmly by, about a mile and a half broad, and the roofs and steeples of Canadian Windsor, on the opposite side, glittered in the white moonlight. It was very pleasant to exchange the shake and rattle of the train for the smooth, easy motion of the boat. We were steered with the greatest precision into the mooring berth on the Canadian side, and the train moved off at once again.

Our road was the Great Western of Canada, and we were very curious to know if the contrast between American and English railroad manners would be very marked.

Well, first, the road bed was rougher than the American one we had just left; jolts and jars were much more frequent; next, though the American stations are wanting as a rule in solidity and cleanliness, in brick and stone, and paint and paper, yet the Canadian ones are far worse. Tumble-down boarding, broken benches, worn platforms, gappy fences everywhere caught the eye. There was a general look of slackness in objects animate and inanimate; a sleepier race of people filled the stations, many of whom seemed to have no business there, not even to "see a friend off." The exception was in the fitly-named London; this place gave the impression of more energy and life and growth.

About midday we neared Niagara, and there left the train.

There was a quiet, old-world look about the place— the railway policeman assisted us to choose a carriage and bargain with the driver to take us to the Falls. A small crowd of idlers took much interest in our start, offering free advice as to where we should go, where stay, where dine.

We turned out of the town, and by a shady road, not being aware how far we had to go, and not knowing that the great river was running near by, unseen at the bottom of its cleft.

We listened, but heard no roar, save that of the train rumbling over the long bridge behind us.

Presently through the trees and bushes lining the road we saw some way off a white gleam, and at the same time a low, dull murmur began to be heard.

Our carriage stopped on the edge of a grassy bit by the road-side, and the driver asked if we would get out. "Get out, why? is this all?" Some way off, across a deep chasm, there were all the buildings of a town—hotels, churches, factories,—and just at their right, and exactly opposite us, was a straight white sheet of falling water, divided into unequal parts by a black rock. "This is the American fall." "Well?" "Won't you get out?" "No." "You had better get out and go to the edge." "No—I tell you; it's humbug—not worth getting out for."

There were three of us—a young English couple, and the writer. While we were looking a heavy thunder shower came almost suddenly up, and the bright sky was clouded over, and the rain pattered on the leaves. It lasted but a few minutes, and the sun shone out once more.

Laughing, we got out and moved a few paces down the road to get a better view. We looked to the right, and laughed no more, for we were in full sight of the Canadian or Horse-shoe Fall—spanned by a rainbow, whether left by the shower, or the daughter of the fall itself, we could not tell.

Deep below our feet was the dark green, almost solid-looking pool in which the American Fall opposite seemed to lose itself without an effort, but bounded at the upper end by the curved wall of waters thundering down the Horseshoe Fall. Just at the left the suspension-bridge spanning the chasm seemed but too light, too ethereal, for the awful height.

Walking down the road still farther we stopped opposite the Prospect House, and from the rock there close to the Fall gazed into the tearing, roaring masses of tortured water, till the effect was graven in the memory never to be forgotten.

Where during the last few years the edge of the centre of the horseshoe has worn or been broken away, the shape of the Fall has become angular instead of rounded. Thus there is an awful corner where the two streams join, where the Spirit of the Falls must live, behind the veil of water revealed as the wind blows to one side or the other the ever-rising foam and mist.

In the vast pool below the colour is dark grass-green, with no sense of light playing on the surface, no reflection from the brown and dusky rocks; in the angle of the Falls the colour is the clearest, most intense emerald green, transparent, limpid, pure. Once seen, the eye seeks always, till there comes the friendly breeze, and the tantalising mist for just one instant moves aside.

Passing still along the road, the reach of river leading to the Falls is seen. Four or five miles wide, broken with rocks, rising everywhere into rapids at the smallest obstacle, the river hurries to its fate, and one feels sympathy almost as if it were a living sentient thing, carried by resistless fate to a fearful doom.

A long solid beam juts out from the land just above the Falls, and by standing on it one can see still farther into the Fall itself; but after a few moments there, one draws back by instinct lest a sudden impulse, a momentary giddiness, even a puff of wind, might carry one away into that awful gulf.

Where in nature is there so strong a contrast as between the green calm luxuriant beauty of the little islands just above the Falls, and the mad brown water hurrying past ? Well may their edges be fenced with strong iron paling, since a slip would carry away any one incautious enough to try to reach the wild flowers, overhanging the brink in lovely masses, to worse than instant death.

An owner of one of these islands had an only son, a boy of twelve. He came home from school in summer time, greeted his parents, and ran out into the garden to renew acquaintance with lawn, and bank, and flowers and ferns. He passed along the bridge on to the little island, fresh and leafy, where he had been hundreds of times before. He was never seen again; no one missed him for many minutes, and then they sought in vain ; they had not even the sad consolations which many find in cherishing, in decking, the place where the bodies of their loved ones rest.

His grave was in that awful whirlpool, where rocks disappear, whence trunks of trees emerge torn and scarred, but which seems to hate to give up the human dead.

Singular the fascination Niagara has for suicides. They come from far to cast themselves in. Shortly before our visit, the wife of a wealthy New York merchant had shown signs of failing intellect. With everything that we most of us crave, "love, obedience, troops

of friends," she left her home, and found her way to
Niagara, tracked by her family, but always having
purpose enough to avoid observation, lose herself in
crowds and evade all pursuit, until she could stand
above that boiling pool and take that plunge.

After a long drive up by the Canadian side, we
returned once again to the Prospect House, after
buying photographs, feather fans, beadwork, and the
rest of the memorials that every one laughs at, but
every one buys.

We climbed to the lookout to bid farewell to
Niagara. The scene can never pass from the memory.
From far off, over the great lakes, rose across the
clear blue sky a solid, black, threatening thunder-
cloud.

It followed down the river towards us, casting a
deep gloom over river and Falls, but leaving a broad
stretch of sunlight on either side, showing clearly the
hills and trees against the blue sky now flecked with
white clouds. Quickly the storm approached, until
the black cloud overhung the Falls.

It was split right through by one flash, which
appeared to begin high over our heads, and bury
itself in the gulf below ; and then the thunder shower

fell, blotting out river, Falls, and sky in one white sheet, while the crashing of the thunder overbore and seemed to quell for one instant the roaring of the Falls.

We could not leave without visiting the rapids below, where the volume of water is crushed together in a narrowed channel until the middle of the river is heaped up, men say, sixteen feet, by the mixed pressure and velocity.

It is right to apologise for saying one word about Niagara, since to most readers it must be assumed to be familiar from their earliest years; still, to pass it by in silence would be almost to insult it. One may not be able to report fully and correctly the conversations of a deep thinker, of a master of some theory in science; and yet if one visited his country and his house, it would be ungracious not to record the fact, and bear witness to his kindly reception.

In the evening we went on again, choosing the New York Central route. We entered the car on the Canadian side, and crossed the great bridge over the rapids, getting our last look up to the Falls.

The distance and the clear, quiet, still evening combined to leave the impression of beauty on our memories, and so to complete the series of changes of effect of which the day had been so full.

A pleasant, chatty American got in with us, and sat down, remarking on the fineness of the evening, the magnificence of the views: he hoped we had been to the various points, and incidentally mentioned the Prospect House. He commented on the way English people spent their money there, and the enormous profits which must be made. He referred to the feather-work, and photographs as being exceptionally dear; and at last quite casually "guessed" we had done as all others do.

Very unsuspectingly, we tossed back the ball of conversation, and concurred in much that he said, but defended the photographs as being both good and not dear.

He asked, "Did you get any of those large views of the Falls? they are the best." "Oh, yes," we answered; "we bought three or four; not mounted, but rolled, for convenience of carriage."

By this time the train was pulling up in the station on the American side, and our friend wished us good-night, and alighted.

In three minutes, back he came with another

fellow as Yankee Custom-house officers, and re-
quested us to hand over our keys. "What for?"
we asked. "Oh, all Canadian works of art and
other manufactures pay duty here."

While we were meditating, our friend went on,
"Have you any other things chargeable besides
those photographs and the feather fans?"

"What is there to pay?" we asked. "A dollar
and a half," said he. "For carrying these trifles
then through the United States territory, to put
them on board ship in three days at New York,
your great Republic fleeces me out of this paltry
sum in this paltry way?" "Yes," he answered.

Whereupon a few winged words passed of a warm
nature. The head man was fetched from his tea,
and the whole matter explained to him before a
small crowd, who did not seem very proud of the
"smartness" of our friend. It ended in our producing the return-ticket to Liverpool by the White
Star line, and the chief's declining to insist on the
payment, much to our first friend's disgust, and we
left them in the heat of controversy.

So much for our last experience of American
custom-houses; begun in bribery and corruption at

New York, it ended with the petty cunning shown
by the insidious scamp we had just left.

The Erie train raced us all the way to Buffalo,
the tracks running side by side, and the pace being
a great deal too lively for the passengers' comfort
or the shareholders' pockets.

So roughly were two friends of ours in the Erie
car treated that the lady told us afterwards that
she was more sick from the jolting than she had
ever been at sea: she was laid up for a day or
two at New York in consequence.

A very crowded night Pullman brought us to
Albany in the early morning.

After breakfasting there we finished the journey
across the continent by the beautiful scenery of the
Hudson River. The last few hours among the
wooded mountains, calm river reaches dotted with
white sails, pretty country houses, and snug villages
of New York State, left us very pleasant memories
of railway travelling in America.

An eight days' passage from Sandy Hook to
Queenstown, marked by no incident and troubled
by no anxiety, fitly closed our travels, and gave us
opportunity to arrange in due order the notes

from which this record of our journey has been compiled.

If this book shall serve to bring more clearly before intending emigrants the risks they run, but the probabilities of success they enjoy, on the other side of the world; if curious readers shall gain truer ideas of the countries being reclaimed from wilderness, of the institutions being tested and developed, of the various problems being worked out there which are of enduring interest for all whose ideas are not bounded by the mill-horse customs of their daily life, then the book will not have been written in vain; and perhaps its many faults, of which no one is more conscious than the writer, may be excused.

ASTORIA, AND MOUTH OF COLUMBIA RIVER.

NOTES TO THE 1976 EDITION

ALTHOUGH MR. NASH wrote primarily for a British audience and his book was published in London, he uses a good many Americanisms, giving the British form also when he felt it necessary. Crackers, he explains, are really biscuits; cross ties on the railroad are sleepers, an elevator is a warehouse, a "slew" is a slough (to rhyme with now), and salal is a type of whortleberry. Corn in England is the equivalent of what Americans call grain. He distinguishes what we call corn as maize, Indian maize, or Indian corn.

He uses variations in spellings of some proper nouns, such as Alkatross for Alcatraz, Menlow for Menlo Park, and Coquelle, Siuselaws, and Umtquas for Indian tribes. For the most part, the reader will have no difficulty in determining his meaning.

Pages x and 43: "Situated only twenty days journey from Liverpool . . ." As indicated on page 43, the Nash party crossed from England to San Francisco in 18 days. If they had left the train in the Sacramento valley on the 17th day, they could have reached western Oregon by rail and stagecoach in three additional days.

Pages xi and 222: The Governor of Oregon was Stephen F. Chadwick, a Democrat who had been Secretary of State and succeeded to the governorship on February 1, 1877, upon the resignation of La Fayette Grover and served in that office until September 11, 1878.

Page 15: The Chicago fire had destroyed 17,450 buildings only six years previously. No wonder the visitor expressed surprise at finding no evidence of the destruction.

Page 27: "lucerne" is a British term for alfalfa.

Page 38: Bret Harte had been gone from California less than a decade. His stories of the gold-mining camps, which apparently were already well known in England, had appeared first in the *Overland Monthly,* which Harte edited—"The Luck of Roaring Camp" in 1868, "The Outcasts of Poker Flat" in 1869, and "The Heathen Chinee" in 1870.

Page 46: Golden Gate Park.

Page 50: In the Appendix of his book, Mr. Nash included a long extract from James Lick's Deeds of Trust, which has been omitted in this reprint as not being of current interest nor pertinent to the main theme of Nash's narrative.

Page 59: Joseph Joachim (1831-1907) was a Hungarian violinist who became a sensation when he p!ayed in London in 1844. Henri F. J. Vieuxtemps (1820-1881) was a Belgian violinist, professor, and composer.

Page 74: This would not have been the present city of San Jose, which is at the opposite—south—end of San Francisco Bay.

Page 76: Nash's trip from San Francisco to The Geysers and back covered a total of about 185 miles. Alkatross (Alcatraz) Island was where one member of the party, Colonel Hogg, had been imprisoned at the close of the Civil War. The "river winding along" would be the Petaluma, and the wharf where they changed to the train would be downstream from the city of Petaluma. As they "steamed gently up the rich valley" they would have passed through the present sites of Santa Rosa, Healdsburg, Geyserville, and Asti to Cloverdale.

Page 78: The Geysers, in the mountains about 15 miles east of Cloverdale, is now the site of the only geothermal power installation in operation in the United States. The 250° F steam is being used to produce nearly as much electricity as all of the other geothermal power insta'lations in the world together. The plant has a rated capacity of 600 megawatts; an addition of 300 megawatts is planned. (*American Scientist,* September-October 1975, pp. 510-521.)

Page 91: The lower end of the McLeod (McCloud) River is now inundated by Shasta Lake.

Page 96: Soda Springs, probably Shasta Springs, just north of Dunsmuir. After completion of the railroad through this canyon, trains regularly stopped here to let passengers refresh themselves at these invigorating springs.

Page 101: The Habersham 1878 map of Oregon shows the villages of Barron, Ash'and, Phoenix (but no Medford) on the way to Jacksonville. Farther north the Stage Road passed through Woodville (now Rogue River) but by-passed Grants Pass.

Page 103: Galesville was near Azalea in Douglas County between Stage Road Pass and Canyonville. Other towns on the Stage Road shown on maps of the time were Myrtle Creek, Roseburg, Winchester, Wilbur, Oakland, Yoncalla, Drain, Creswell, and Eugene City.

Page 104: "head of the Rogue" should be Umpqua. In speaking of corn in this passage, Nash probably means all sorts of grain crops.

Page 107: From Roseburg, Nash and his companions went by rail to Albany. A businessman by the name of Crawford drove them eight miles to Corvallis. (*General Report,* p. 4)

Page 109: Oregon has grown a little since 1877. At present the size is given as 96,209 square miles as compared with the 95,274 given by Nash.

Page 110: Mount Pitt was the name used from 1843 to 1905 for the peak northeast of Medford, which previously and subsequently was known as Mount McLoughlin.

Pages 111: The map in the endpapers of this book, taken from Nash's 1878 book, shows the Portland-Roseburg railroad, the line "in progress on the western side," and the route of what later became the proposed Corvallis and Eastern Railroad—from Yaquina Bay to Corvallis and Albany and up the North Santiam valley to the summit of the Cascades. Along the Crooked River it would have passed near Prineville, a village at the time, and Camp Harney north of the present site of Burns, and finally down the Owyhee valley to the Snake River.

Page 120: Ellensburg is the former name for Gold Beach.

Pages 124, 126-127: The Willamette Valley and Cascade Mountains Military Road used the Santiam Pass in crossing the Cascades and was projected on through eastern Oregon along the route of the proposed Corvallis and Eastern.

Page 133: The "large, red-brick school-house" would be the center section of the Philomath College bui'ding, which had been in use for ten years. The east and west wings were not added until 1905 and 1907. Enrollment in 1874-75 was 20 college-level students and 52 in the preparatory and 48 in the primary departments. The college ceased to operate as an educational institution in 1929. The building, which is now on the National Register of Historic Places, is being restored.

Page 139: The "expedition" included the three Englishmen—Nash, Mose'ey, and Kerr; Colonel Hogg and the Co'onel's brother William Hoag; George Mercer, a county surveyor who had made the original surveys of much of the wagon-road lands they were going to see; and Edwin Alden "Kit" Abbey, a sometime resident of Corvallis and of Elk City, where he was the first postmaster. Abbey's younger brother, Peter M., was the proprietor of the Bay View House (Abbey House), a hotel in Newport. The made-to-order cook stove and luggage were carried in a wagon driven by the college student who had volunteered to cook for them.

Page 142: The camp on the Luckiamute River may have been near the present sawmill and store in King's Valley, where there was a sawmill and a grist mill at the time, or at Hoskins where there was a smaller mill.

Page 143: For probable location of the Meade farmhouse, see note for page 165.

Pages 146-147: Fort Hoskins was on the Luckiamute River near the mouth of Bonner Creek in southwestern King's Valley. Captain Christopher C. Augur established it for the U.S. Army on July 26, 1856, and named it for Charles Hoskins, a lieutenant killed in the battle of Monterrey, Mexico, ten years previously. The purpose of the fort was to guard the pass through the Coast Range between the Willamette Valley and concentration of Indians at the Siletz Agency. 2nd Lt. Philip H. Sheridan spent part of a year at Fort Hoskins and built a trail over the Coast Range into the Indian reservation. Capt. Frederick T. Dent, a brother-in-law of General Ulysses S. Grant, commanded Fort Hoskins for a while after Augur was transferred in 1861. Augur and Sheridan became major generals and Dent a brigadier general in the Civil War. After the regular Army troops were transferred to other Civil War assignments, the fort was manned by volunteers from California, Washington, and Oregon until it was closed on April 13, 1865. (See *A Webfoot Volunteer* edited by Nelson and Onstad and *Oregon Geographic Names*, 4th edition, by Lewis L. McArthur. Portland: Oregon Historical Society, 1974, pp. 284-285, 369.

Page 147: For probable location of the Wilcox and Trapp farms see note for page 165.

Page 156: The "very tall, bearded man, about fifty-five" may have been Thomas Condon, the minister-geologist and popular lecturer who had just completed his first year on the first faculty of the University of Oregon. Condon was bearded and 55 at the time and, according to his biographer, his daughter Ellen Condon McCornack, he was

at Yaquina Bay before July 26 that summer. The family
camped at the mouth of Nye Brook, which is within the
present city of Newport. It would have been in keeping
with the character and practices of Professor Condon to
have delivered the lecture Nash describes. In later years,
Nash became well acquainted with the work of this pioneer
geologist. (*Thomas Condon: Pioneer Geologist of Oregon.*
Eugene: The University Press, 1928, pp. 181, 209, 341-
342.)

Page 158: "Depot Slew (Slough)" empties into the Yaquina
River at Toledo. See note for page 165.

Page 165: Nash's narrative of the trip to the coast varies
somewhat from that of Henry Moseley in the *General
Report* and from what Nash later wrote in *Two Years in
Oregon* and in *A Lawyer's Life on Two Continents.* James
A. Blodgett of Corvallis, who was born in the valley Nash
describes on pages 200-204 and whose great-grandfather,
William Blodgett, was the first settler there, has studied
these various texts. Using his knowledge of the region he
grew up in and after tracing the land records of Benton
County, Mr. Blodgett has come to these conclusions:

"The expedition of seven horsemen and a cook driving
a cook wagon left Corvallis on the afternoon of July 12,
1877, and camped that night near Philomath (p. 139). On
the 13th, they camped in Kings Valley (p. 142). On the
14th they camped at Meade's (pp. 143, 144), which
was probably at what is now called Nortons on the Yaquina
west of Nashville. A man named Meade owned 160 acres
there. This location is west of the divide which Nash tells
of crossing on page 146.

"In *Oregon: There and Back in 1877* Nash implies that
the party all traveled the same road. According to what
he later wrote, it appears that Nash, possibly accompanied
by Kit Abbey, left the others on the wagon road and took
a trail that led toward Siletz. In *Two Years in Oregon,*
p. 127, Nash says, 'To get [from] King's Valley . . . we
had to take the mountain-trail first cut out by General
Sheridan, twenty years ago.' In *A Lawyer's Life on Two*

Continents, p. 191, he writes, 'In 1877 I was one of the party that found its way . . . by King's Valley . . . to the watershed between the Willamette and the Siletz. It was a very rough trail . . . overgrown since General Sheridan as a young lieutenant . . . cut it out . . . At the very head of the watershed we halted . . . At our feet several miles away lay a green valley in the heart of the wilderness. We judged it to be of many hundred acres in extent . . . not obstructed by green timber, old or young . . . The road led us down to and through it from end to end, and we followed the main creek [Little Rock Creek] along till it joined the Siletz River.'

"Mentioning this side trip is significant because soon after the Nashes moved to Oregon in 1879, Wallis filed for a homestead on one 640-acre section in this green valley in the heart of the wilderness. Later he homesteaded a second section, which it was possible to do at that time, and purchased the "school" section that lay between. In this way he gained title to sections 15, 16, and 17, in township 10 S, range 8 W. This is where he built his country home and where his family grew up, the home he retired to in later years and where he died in 1926. Ownership of part of this property remained in the family until it was sold in 1966.

"One may surmise that on the 1877 trip, Nash and Abbey, if that is who was with him, followed Little Rock Creek as far as Logsden, then returned part way to go up over the open ridge and rejoin the others at Meade's (Nortons). Moseley is specific that crossing of the divide was made at Summit and that they spent the night of July 14 at Meade's.

"As a boy, I knew this country well. A great fire in 1850, while my great-grandfather was in California, destroyed about 150 square miles of virgin forest. The fire stopped along a line approximately from Hoskins to Blodgett to Marys Peak. What is again dense forest was, in 1877, open fern-covered ground interspersed with the skeletons of burned trees. Burnt Woods takes its name from this feature. Note the charred remnants of tall trees and the returning vegetation in Mr. Nash's drawing of Elk City, opposite page 194.

"Trapp's (p. 147) was two miles above Eddy's grist mill (Eddyville) at the junction of the Little Elk and the Yaquina, according to Nash in *Two Years in Oregon*, p. 58. I could not find a land deed recorded for Trapp.

"The camp on the 15th, Moseley says, was at Wilcox's (p. 147), which would be near where Thornton Creek enters the Yaquina. The next day, we may again surmise, was when their 'cavalcade of seven horses' (p. 194) made a noon stop at Elk City (sometimes called Yaquina), which was the western terminus of the wagon road.

"The runaway (pp. 147-148), must have occurred on the 16th between Elk City and Newport, and they must have seen the Pacific soon after overtaking Moseley. They arrived in Newport late that afternoon.

"The party stayed in Newport the nights of July 16 and 17, attending the lecture one night and the dance the other night. On the 18th they rode to the Siletz Indian reservation, following the road along Depot S'ough (p. 158). The settler who told them about the coal seam was probably the Mr. Towner who owned property near Olalla Slough a little to the east.

"On the evening of the 18th they visited the Agency Doctor and the Indian Agent and on the 19th and 20th camped south of Siletz. Nash, Moseley, Mercer, and Towner went coal-seeking on foot and undoubtedly left their horses in camp. Moseley says he inspected the coal seam on the 20th and thought it was in section 24 or 25 (T 10 S, R 11 W), but it may have been in section 13 to the north. They rejoined the others about 5 p.m. on the 20th.

"On the return trip, instead of following their previous route, they turned right at Eddyville and went up Little Elk Creek and along the present-day route of highway U.S. 20. On July 21 they camped at the farm of Mr. Fleckenger (the Sluggard, pp. 196-200) on Shotpouch Creek (Burnt Woods).

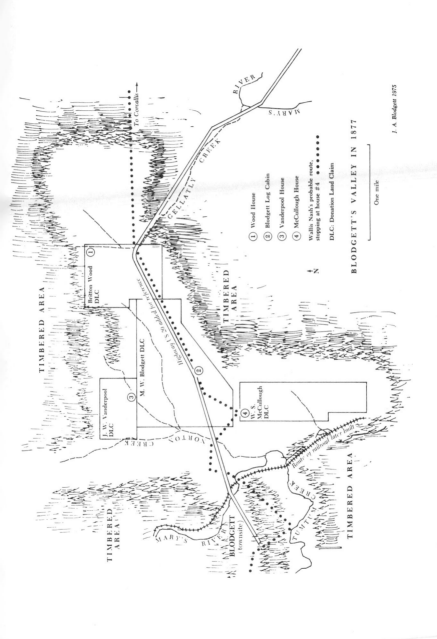

BLODGETT'S VALLEY IN 1877

① Wood House
② Blodgett Log Cabin
③ Vanderpool House
④ McCullough House

Wallis Nash's probable route,
stopping at house #4 ●●●●●●

DLC: Donation Land Claim

N

One mile

J. A. Blodgett 1975

"On the 22nd 'the view of a lovely valley [Blodgett's] opened out' (p. 200). There were four Donation Land Claims in this valley at the time (see map). Only one had passed to a buyer. That would be the first one they came to from the west and 'the most distant farm at the farther end of the valley' (p. 201) in reference to Corvallis. If we have correctly identified the house where they stopped, Nash would have talked with Henry P. McCullough, who had purchased the farm in 1873. This McCullough was no relation to the original W. S. McCullough who had taken the Donation Land Claim. The McCullough house remained standing until it burned down in 1974. It was unoccupied at the time, but the well of cold water was still usable and roses and honeysuckle still covered the south and west sides.

"One difficulty in tracing early ownership of property in this area is that settlers often neglected the recording of deeds. While most of them staked out their claims and paid the registration fees promptly, they took their time about getting the final patent from the Land Office. Records show that my own great-grandfather waited nearly 40 years before he applied for the deed to his Donation Land Claim. The deed is the only local record.

"In Blodgett's Valley, the party had come back to the wagon road that would take them through Wren and Philomath to Corvallis. The only part of the wagon road that had not been inspected, apparently, was the sector between Blodgett and Summit. Moseley mentions 'an excursion up Marys Peak,' however, and there may have been other side trips that neither author mentions."

Page 188: This would have been one of the mills at Albany (possibly that of Thomas Montieth) on the Willamette River using the power canal that brought water 14 miles from the South Santiam River near Lebanon.

Page 200: Blodgett's Valley. See previous note and map.

Page 204: This is Nash's first mention of the Oregon Agricultural College to which he gave unstinted support in later years. See note for page 218 and the personal notes.

Page 212: The historian of Oregon newspapers, George S. Turnbull, says that the *Crucible* was a weekly published in Philomath rather than in Corvallis. In 1877, Dr. John B. Horner, later professor and museum curator at Oregon State College, was editor of this first newspaper published in Philomath. His partner, possibly the "sub-editor" Nash met, was J. C. Leasure. The subscription price was $2.50 a year and the circulation about 250. A member of the Philomath College faculty became editor the next year, but the paper soon died of what Turnbull calls "malnutrition." (*History of Oregon Newspapers,* pp. 232-233.)

Page 214: The Willamette University Medical School was chartered in 1865. Classes were first held in Portland but in 1867 the school was moved to Salem, where ten years later it was in the condition Mr. Nash describes. It remained in Salem until 1913, when it was moved back to Portland and united with the University of Oregon Medical School. Pharmacy courses had been added at Oregon Agricultural College in 1898, and the School of Pharmacy for the state was established there in 1917.

Page 217: The "principal" Nash talked to would have been the college president, B. L. Arnold, A. M., Professor of Moral Philosophy and Physics.

Page 218: The "large wooden bui'ding in the outskirts of town" was on the block bounded by 5th, Madison, 6th, and Monroe streets. The 1875-76 Annual Catalog for the college lists 51 students in the Agricultural Department and 147 in the Collegiate Department. As Nash points out, the college had been designated in 1868 to receive the benefits of a grant of 90,000 acres of public lands under the provisions of the Morrill Act of 1862, but the Columbia Conference of the Methodist Episcopal Church, South, continued to manage and support the college, as it had done since 1860 and would continue to do until 1885.

After the state took control of Corvallis College in 1885, local citizens, who by that time included the Nash family, raised money to build what is now Benton Hall on the Oregon State University campus. Mr. Nash served on the new Board of Regents, as temporary chairman in 1886 and as secretary until the end of 1894. He retired from the Board in 1898. He actively supported the establishment of the Agricultural Experiment Station in 1888. He and Mrs. Nash were largely responsible for finding, interviewing, and bringing to Corvallis Dr. Margaret Snell as the first Professor of Household Economy and Hygiene (Home Economics) on the west coast. In many other respects Oregon State University still shows the early influence of the Nashes, and Nash Hall commemorates their name.

Page 219: Dr. J. C. Hawthorne built the first non-military hospital in Oregon in East Portland in 1861. Located at S.E. 12th and Asylum (now Hawthorne) streets, it became primarily a home for the insane, who were cared for under contract from the state until the state asylum was built in Salem in 1883. (*The Doctor in Oregon,* pp. 510-511.)

Page 220: The railroad distance from Salem to Portland is only half of the 100 miles given by Nash.

Page 222: William Hoag accompanied Nash to Salem to call on Governor Chadwick and on to the land office in Oregon City, while Colonel Hogg, Moseley, and Kerr followed the proposed route of the railroad over the Cascade Mountains and across eastern Oregon. (*General Report,* p. 13.)

Page 223: Manufacturing began at Oregon City in 1846, when Dr. John McLoughlin, former factor for the Hudson's Bay Company at Fort Vancouver, built a grist mill.

Page 225: The first paper mill at Oregon City was built in 1866. The production of one ton of paper daily that Nash mentions (but which is questionable) has grown, in the two huge plants that dominate both sides of Willamette Falls, to 1,200 tons a day.

Page 237: Mr. Nash errs in identifying the hotel that burned down as the Metropolitan. There was a Metropolis Hotel in Portland at the time, but it was the Cosmopolitan that caught fire at 2 a.m. on Saturday, July 25, 1877.

Thomas Perkins was the man who lost his life. Eighty others lost their residences. "The new buildings of a news-paper-office, within a few feet of the blazing hotel," were those of the *Morning Oregonian* (see issue of Monday, July 27, 1877).

Page 244: The pilings on which Nash observed Astoria being bui't continued in use for decades, and the open spaces around them made excellent flues to spread the fire that destroyed 32 city blocks in two days in early December 1922.

Page 247: "pine-clad" hills. Unfamiliar with the new species, Douglas-fir, early visitors often mistook it for a pine. It was sometimes called "Oregon pine."

Page 257: Brigham Young died on August 29, 1877.

Personal Notes

Mr. Nash says nothing about his personal life in this narrative, but because the reader will be interested, a few more notes seem appropriate. Dr. Gwyneth Britton of the Oregon State University faculty made some inquiries in England and among Nash's descendants and has pro-vided some of the following information.

Wallis Nash, the son of Searle James Nash and Eliza-beth Webb Nash, was born in Surrey County, England, on August 16, 1837, the year Victoria became Queen. In one of the few published comments about himself, Nash wrote:

"I was an only son, and was blessed with a stepmother who did her best to fill the place of the mother who was taken when I was but a year-old infant. My father and I lived in the home of my stepmother's father, Dr. John Pye-Smith, who was the author of *Scripture and Geology,* and of *The Scripture Testimony to the Messiah,* and other controversial books dating from the early decades of the nineteenth century. His book shelves were full. Looking back, I see that my step-grandfather was a broader minded and more truly scholarly man than I believed during my early years. At any rate, my young years were fed on books.

"My father being a Nonconformist, and a Congregationalist, the great schools of England—Eton, Harrow, Winchester, and the rest, and the old universities, Oxford, Cambridge and Durham—were closed to me. . . . To give me the best chance possible, I was sent to Mill Hill School, the best of its time founded by nonconformists, and even in its early years beginning to accumulate traditions of nation-wide names of its pupils." (*A Lawyer's Life on Two Continents*, p. 14.)

The records of Mill Hill School show that Wallis Nash attended that school from January 1849 to June 1852, that he was a "keen musician," that he later presented a singing prize to the school, that he served both as a Trustee and a Life Governor of the school, and that his stepmother's father had been a cofounder of the school.

Following study at the University of London, Nash lived in the country for a year, recuperating from symptoms of tuberculosis. After an apprenticeship in law offices in several towns, he joined Field and Roscoe in London. Young Al'an Field of that firm and Nash bought out another firm of solicitors and formed Nash and Field, which is still in existence as Nash Field & Co., 9 Devereux Court, London WC2R. The partners since 1972 have been Hedley J. Newton, Edward Tolley Grubb, Henry J. K. Burne, and John Trevor Hilling. (Records Department, Law Society's Hall, December 1975.)

Nash married Annie Budget in 1866. She died in 1869 at the time of the birth of their son, Wallis Gifford.

Nash's second wife, whom he married in 1871, was Louisa A'Humity Desborough. To them were born a total of nine children, three girls and six boys. Ruth, Vivian, Oscar, and Oliver died of what Nash called "virulent scarlet fever" in 1877. Desborough, Percival, Dorothea, and their half-brother Wallis Gifford accompanied their parents to Oregon in 1879. Two more sons, Louis Darwin and Roderic, were born in Corvallis.

In making the exodus from England to Oregon, the Nashes were accompanied by what he calls "a motley company." In addition to their three boys and baby girl, there were a nurse for the baby, a cook, a cousin who had been a highlander guardsman, a newly married young couple, and four boys whose relatives made a "moderate monthly payment" to Nash to help support them as long as they remained under his control. On May 17, 1879, they arrived in Corvallis by river steamer from Portland. "The season was unusually late," Nash later wrote, "and the streets of the little town were ankle deep in mud, crossed by planks a foot wide." After a few days in a hotel they moved into a large house Colonel Hogg had prepared for them on the site where Waldo Hall on the Oregon State University campus now stands. Thus began their adventures in the new world.

Descendants of Wallis Nash and his first wife, Annie Budget, total five. Those of Wallis and Louisa A. Desborough Nash number 38, including the four children who died in England. Of this total of 43 descendants, 30 are believed to be still living. Several step-children and many spouses of the descendants are also now included in this burgeoning family.

Bibliography

General Report on Journey to Oregon and Details of Purchase of Land by Wallis Nash, Henry N. Moseley, and Francis E. Kerr. London: Edward Stanford, 1877.

Oregon: There and Back in 1877 by Wallis Nash. London: Macmillan and Co., 1878.

Oregon: Its Resources, Climate, People, and Productions by H. N. Moseley. London: Howard Stanford, 1878.

Two Years in Oregon by Wallis Nash. New York: D. Appleton and Company, 1882.

Farm, Ranch, and Range in Oregon by Wallis Nash. Portland: Lewis and Clark Centennial Commission, 1904.

The Settler's Handbook to Oregon by Wallis Nash. Portland: The J. K. Gill Co., 1904.

A Lawyer's Life on Two Continents by Wallis Nash. Boston: The Gorham Press, 1919.

History of the Oregon Country by Harvey W. Scott, vol. IV. Cambridge: The Riverside Press, 1924.

Thomas Condon: Pioneer Geologist of Oregon by Ellen Condon McCornack. Eugene, Oregon: at the University Press, 1928.

History of Oregon Newspapers by George S. Turnbull. Portland: Binfords and Mort, 1939.

The Doctor in Oregon, a Medical History by O. Larsell. Portland: Oregon Historical Society, 1947.

A Webfoot Volunteer: The Diary of William M. Hilleary 1864-1866 edited by Herbert B. Nelson and Preston E. Onstad. Corvallis: Oregon State University Press, 1965. Published in cooperation with the Oregon Historical Society.

A MAP
OF
OREGON

Scale of English Miles.

0   10   20   40   60   80   100